Did the Bible Really Come From God?

FIRST PRINTING

Billy Crone

Cover Design:
Get A Life Media

To my brother, Jim.

As I look back on this life,
I am amazed and humbled at the manifold wisdom of God.
What I mean is this.
Of all the people that the Lord would ordain to overshadow me,
via an only older brother,
it was and is you.

Thank you for the sharing of your time,
your patience, your wisdom, and very life in me.
It has proven to be an investment in God's hands,
to help mold me into a responsible man.

At times, you have been more than a brother to me,
but a father figure as well, when I needed it most.
Thank you, Jim.
I love you.

Contents

Preface

When I was a "brand new" Christian I was busy doing what I figured *all* Christians should do and that is, witnessing. I was learning new and exciting information each day as I had enrolled in Bible College eight weeks after being saved. One day, I was engaged in a conversation with my brother Jim concerning the Book of Genesis and the conditions of the Garden of Eden prior to the fall of man. As we continued to talk, I was challenged with the classical response of, "How do I know it's true?" This hit me like a ton of bricks. I knew the Bible was God's Word but this was the first time that I was asked for "proof." I stumbled through the rest of the conversation and left shortly thereafter. That night I prayed a prayer that changed the course of this life. I cried out, "God, I don't want to be a 'copycat Christian.' I do not want to merely repeat or 'copy' what I learn about the Scriptures from my instructors, even though I do not doubt their integrity, but I want to know for myself, *why I believe what I believe*." From then on, I began to not only study the truth of God's Word but to understand it from all angles, skeptic and non-skeptic alike. This has proven to be a powerful force in enabling God to use this life right on up to today in "giving a reason for the hope that lies within me."

Now, even though this is clearly a mandate for all believers to fulfill, I have noticed that over the years, although there are volumes of apologetic books out there to equip the Christian to give a proper defense and aid them in effective witnessing, many people still will not pick them up. Some might buy one or two in their lifetime but they seem have a hard time in reading them due to the "technical" language that is by necessity contained within. The constant complaint seems to be "It's too hard to understand. It's too boring." Therefore, the purpose of this book is not to merely hand you yet another apologetic book on popular questions raised by the skeptic concerning the Bible, but one that is *easy* to understand and follow, and believe it or not, actually *fun* to read! My desire is that you will not only finish this book, but that you would join me in a passionate pursuit of God's truth and share it with every soul that the Lord would put in your path. One last piece of advice. When you are through reading this book then will you please READ YOUR BIBLE? I mean that in the nicest possible way. Enjoy, and I'm looking forward to seeing you someday!

Billy Crone
Las Vegas, Nevada
2018

Chapter One

The Bible Says So

I hope this doesn't come as a surprise to you, but how many of you know that even Christians make mistakes once in awhile? Uh huh! It really does happen! And for those of you who don't believe me, I've got some proof. That's right! We're going to look at some actual Church Bulletin Bloopers and you tell me if we Christians aren't human once in a while! These were printed right here in America.

• The ladies of the Church have cast off clothing of every kind. They may be seen in the basement on Friday afternoon.

• Attend this week's conference and you will hear an excellent speaker and heave a healthy lunch.

• The church will host an evening of fine dining, superb entertainment, and gracious hostility.

• Low Self-Esteem Support Group will meet Thursday at 7 to 8:30 p.m. Please use the back door.

• For the pancake breakfast next Saturday, the Pastor would appreciate it if the ladies of the congregation would lend him their electric girdles.

• The Associate Minister unveiled the Church's new stewardship campaign slogan last Sunday: "I Upped My Pledge - Up Yours."

• Next Sunday Mrs. Vinson will be soloist for the morning service. The pastor will then speak on "It's a Terrible Experience."

• Barbara remains in the hospital and needs blood donors for more transfusions. She is also having trouble sleeping and requests tapes of Pastor Jack's sermons.

• This Christmas season smile at someone who is hard to love and say "hell" to those who don't care much about you.

• Our concluding song on Christmas Day is "Angels We Have Heard Get High."

Now as you can see, even we Christians unfortunately make mistakes, don't we? But I hope there's one mistake as a Christian that we never make and that is this: To doubt that the Bible really did come from God. I say it again, to doubt that the Bible really came from God. And I say that because many people in our world today are in a frantic search for truth. It doesn't matter anymore because it is spilling out all over the place because of world events. Christian, non-Christian, it doesn't matter, everybody recognizes that something is horribly wrong with our world and it's getting worse. It doesn't matter what we say, what we do, how we vote, our world continues to spiral down out of control. And so, many people, not just Christians are seeking answers to questions of life, like; 'Can we have true and lasting peace in this world? Why is there so much evil and suffering? Why has all this shooting been going on? Where did all this evil come from? And is there any hope?' And the irony is, all this searching for answers is actually a good thing because it's starting to wake people up, to start focusing on eternal things, which is good. But the problem is, they are looking in all the wrong places for the answers to these questions. They're actually hoping that somebody, somewhere, will dig up some ancient text that will unlock all the secrets to life. Or they're actually hoping that somehow, someway, a supposed alien, with a higher intelligence, will land on planet earth and solve all of our problems. Or as the X-Files puts it, "The Truth is Out There," right? That's what people believe. But what if I were to tell you that the X-Files is right! Yeah, the truth is out there, it's right under our noses. It's called the Bible. But the problem is nobody will pick it up. Its actually collecting dust in virtually every home in America.

• Among households which own a Bible, the typical count is three Bibles per household.

• Almost every household in America (92%) owns at least one copy of the Christian Bible. This includes most homes in which the adults are not practicing Christians as well as the homes of hundreds of thousands of atheists. Even they have a copy of the Bible![1]

Yeah, the truth is out there, but the irony is, it's collecting dust in virtually every home in America. And so that brings me to the question, "Why?" Why is it that people refuse to pick up the Bible when they're in such a frantic search for truth because of world events? And it's actually collecting dust.

It's right out there in the open! I think it's due to two things. One, it's due to a century or more of skepticism and false criticism towards the Bible. That it really did come from God. So, people don't pick it up because they think it didn't come from God, that it was just a book whooped up by man filled with contradictions and errors. And two, it's also because of the hypocritical behavior of the

Christian community who on the one hand says, "Oh yeah, the Bible really did come from God, and you need to read it to find the answers you're looking for", but the problem is we never pick it up either! And they see us. And apparently, we send a loud message to them, it's not that important. Is it really that bad? That Christians aren't picking up their Bible. Is it really that bad? How do I know? Because when it comes to our Biblical knowledge, I think it's a little lacking. Don't believe me? Just ask these kids.

• Lot's wife was a pillar of salt by day, but a ball of fire by night.

• The Fifth Commandment is to humor thy mother and father.

• Moses died before he ever reached the UK. Then, Joshua led the Hebrews in the Battle of Geritol.

• The greatest miracle in the Bible is when Joshua told his son to stand still and he obeyed him.

• David was a Hebrew king and fought with the Finkelsteins.

• Solomon, one of David's sons, had 300 wives and 700 porcupines.

• When the three wise guys from the East Side arrived, they found Jesus in the manager. Jesus was born because Mary had an immaculate contraption.

• Jesus enunciated the Golden Rule, which says to do one to others before they do one to you. He also explained, "Man doth not live by sweat alone."

• One of the opossums was St. Matthew, who was by profession a taximan.

• A Christian should have only one wife. This is called monotony.

Now that's kind of funny, but how many of you would say those kids probably could use a little refresher course on their Biblical knowledge there, you know what I'm saying? Uh, slightly! But that's right, believe it or not, even we Christian adults don't fare much better. Don't believe me? Check out these stats on Christian adults and their knowledge of the Bible and you tell me how well we're doing.

• 80% of Christians say the Bible teaches, "That God helps those who help themselves."

• 12% say the name of Noah's wife was Joan of Arc.

• 49% say the Bible teaches that money is the root of all evil.

• 50% of Christians say there is no absolute truth.

• 55% of Christians say the Bible has errors in it.

• 47% don't have a commitment to the Christian faith as a top priority.

• 58% don't have being active in a local church as one of their top goals in life.

• 35% of Christians say that to get by in life these days, sometimes you have to bend the rules for your own benefit.

• 49% of Pastors no longer have a Biblical worldview.

• 93% of Christians no longer have a Biblical worldview.[2]

Those kids that thought that David was fighting with the Finklesteins in the battle of Geritol, and Solomon had a bunch of porcupines, they are going to become the next generation, which means that it's only going to get worse when it comes to knowledge and the understanding of the Bible. I wonder what kind of "Christian Adults" they're going to be? And here's the point. I don't know about you, but I am completely aghast at those stats. I mean, think about it. Why didn't all those Christians have a 100% agreement on the accuracy of the Bible? I mean, of all people who should never doubt that the Bible really did come from God, it should be Christians, right? But that's not what we see! Even Christians are doubting that the Bible really did come from God! And that's why, to stave off this criticism and hypocrisy even in the Church, we're going to jump right in and ask the question, "Did the Bible Really Come from God?" And what we're going to do is take a look at the Ten Lines of Solid Logical Evidence that the Bible really did come from God. And when we're done, you're going to see that it *had* to come from God. There is no way in the world man, even on his best day could ever whip up something like we see in the scripture. It's unlike any other book on the planet.

The **1st line of evidence** showing us that the Bible really did come from God is that the **Bible says so.** But don't take my word for it. Let's take a look at what God tells us about this book. Was it really whooped up by man, who wrote this thing, how did it come about? Paul is giving a final charge to Timothy, more than likely this book was written toward the end of Paul's life. He is laying it on the line to young Timothy if Paul isn't going to be around, he is letting him know what the most important thing for him is to focus on, and that is what we read.

2 Timothy 3:10-17 "You, however, know all about my teaching, my way of life, my purpose, faith, patience, love, endurance, persecutions, sufferings – what kinds of things happened to me in Antioch, Iconium and Lystra, the persecutions I endured. Yet the Lord rescued me from all of them. In fact, anyone who wants to live a godly life in Christ Jesus will be persecuted, while evil men and impostors will go from bad to worse, deceiving and being deceived. But as for you, continue in what you have learned and have become convinced of, because you know those from whom you learned it, and how from infancy you have known the Holy Scriptures, which are able to make you wise for salvation through faith in Christ Jesus. All Scripture is God breathed and is useful for teaching, rebuking, correcting and training in righteousness, so that the man of God may be thoroughly equipped for every good work."

So how do we know that the Bible really did come from God? Well, what did we just read? The 1st line of evidence is that the Bible says so. And believe it or not, this is a very important factor. You see, if anyone is in a genuine search to validate a document they must first give that document the benefit of the doubt, right? Even Aristotle knew this when he said:

"The benefit of the doubt is to be given to the document itself, and not arrogated by the critic to himself."

This is the problem. This is what the skeptics do today. They do just the opposite. They assume the Bible is full of errors until it's proven absolutely genuine. They've got it totally backwards. Even in our court rooms we know that someone's innocent until proven guilty, right? Therefore, if you're honest in your approach towards the Bible and if it really came from God, shouldn't the same standard be applied to validating the Bible to see if it came from God? Of course! So, let's do that. Let's see what the

Bible has to say about it being the Word of God.

- "The Lord hath spoken" – 30 times
- "It is written" – 80 times
- "The word of the Lord" – 258 times
- "Thus, saith the Lord" – 415 times
- "Saith the Lord" – 854 times

And that's not all of them. That's just a sampling! But as you can see, hundreds and hundreds of times, the Bible simply and emphatically declares that it literally did come from God! So, here's the point. You have to give it the benefit of the doubt like Aristotle said, that if it says it came from God, then maybe it really did come from God, right? And think about the hypocrisy here. Why is it that no honest scholar treats any other ancient document in the same hypocritical manner that the skeptics do with the Bible? Why do they assume it's wrong right off the bat? Why don't they give it the benefit of the doubt that since it claims to be from God that it might really be from God? Wouldn't that be the honest place to start? But usually the skeptics will object and say something like this, "Well, that's just circular reasoning! One book declaring itself to be from God, that's ludicrous. That's exactly what you'd expect by a book whooped up by man." That's precisely the point. The Bible is not just one book whooped up by man! It's a collection of 66 books written by many different men, in many different time periods, who didn't even know each other, proving that it had to come from God! Man couldn't make this thing up! Don't believe me? Check out these amazing facts on the Bible.

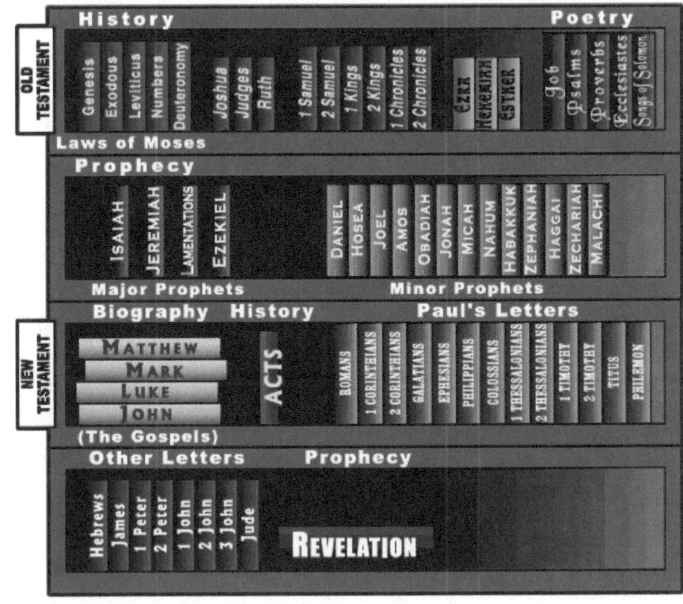

• Written over a 1,500-year span.

• Written over 40 generations.

• Written by more than 40 authors, from every walk of life – including kings, peasants, philosophers, fishermen, poets, statesmen, scholars, etc.

• Written in different places, wilderness, dungeons, palaces, etc.

• Written at different times, times of war and times of peace, etc.

• Written during different moods, from heights of joy and from the depths of despair, etc.

• Written on three different continents, Asia, Africa, and Europe.

• Written in three different languages, Hebrew, Aramaic, and Greek.

• And it never once contradicts itself and it has the same message through and through!

What? Man, on his best day, could never whoop up something like that! It proves that it had to come from God! And yet even with all these amazing characteristics showing that the Bible really did come from God, just like He says over and over again, people will still turn to other supposed sources of truth to find their answers.

The **1st faulty source of truth** that people turn to instead of the Bible is **Worldly False Prophets.** This is crazy! God wants us to know the truth and that's why He gave us the Bible. And that's why He tells us in the Bible to not listen to these guys, they're going to lie to you!

Deuteronomy 18:9-12 "When you enter the land the LORD your God is giving you, do not learn to imitate the detestable ways of the nations there. Let no one be found among you who sacrifices his son or daughter in the fire, who practices divination or sorcery, interprets omens, engages in witchcraft, or casts spells, or who is a medium or spiritist or who consults the dead. Anyone who does these things is detestable to the LORD."

Why? Because it's demonic and God doesn't want you to be lied to! He told us over and over again that the Bible came from Him and we just need to stick to it, so we can know the truth! And yet people today still turn to these same lying demonic spirits to get their source of truth. Don't believe me? Let's take a look at some of the most popular ones out there today. The first one is Nostradamus. Michael Nostradamus was a 16th century French physician and astrologer. He wrote four-line verses called "quatrains" that many of his modern-day followers see as proof that he was a true prophet. Really? Let's put him to the test. Here's just one example of his extremely vague quatrains.

The year 1999 seven months.
From the sky will come the great King of Terror.
To resuscitate the great king of the Mongols.
Before and after, Mars reigns by good luck.
At forty-five degrees the sky will burn.
Fire to approach the great new city.
In an instant a great scattered flame will leap up.
When one will want to demand proof of the Normans.

Nostradamus's supporters have retrospectively claimed that he predicted major world events, including the Great Fire of London, the French Revolution the rises of Napoleon Bonaparte and Adolf Hitler, the atomic bombings of Hiroshima and Nagasaki, and the September 11 attacks.

Well, there you have it, believe it or not, according to the experts, Nostradamus just predicted 9-11. And even when you call them on that insane view they will usually say something like, "Well, 1999 is not "too far off" from 2001. And the references to fire and terror from the sky "sounds" like an aerial attack. New York City is "close" to 45 degrees latitude," (Actually it's about 40.) And then they of course don't mention who in the world was "The great king of the Mongols" and what does this have to do with the planet "Mars" and who on the 9-11 commission actually demanded proof from the "Normans?" And neither do they mention that "the great new city" spoken of by Nostradamus in original French was "Villeneuve," which is the name of a town outside of Paris, which is near a 45 degrees latitude. And yet Nostradamus is more popular than ever. Immediately following the September 11 attacks, his books climbed to the top of Amazon.com's sellers list, and it shot off bookstore shelves all around the country. And yet, it is well documented that Nostradamus received these supposed prophetic quatrains using a combination of astrology, divination, and guidance from an angelic spirit (demon). He used various forms of meditation focusing on fire or water while being under the influence of mild hallucinogens which is a common practice used by witches even today. It's called scrying! Scrying is a practice used by witches to concentrate on an object until visions appear. And believe it or not, Nostradamus not only knew he was messing with dangerous occult practices, but he even warned his own son not to follow his footsteps because he knew he was headed to hell!

"He beseeched his infant son never to dabble in such practices for, he says, they desiccate (or dry up) the body, disturb the mind, and send the soul to perdition. For that reason, he burned to ashes the ancient books that he had learned these techniques from and when he did, he said they burned with an unnatural brilliance."

And I'm going to listen to him over the Word of God in the Bible? Oh, but he's not the only false prophet people unfortunately buy into. As we all just recently found out, the "Mayan Prophecy of 2012" was not only not true, but it was nothing more than wild speculations over the Mayan calendar. The only thing that ended was the Mayan calendar system. In fact, even though people said the Mayans were predicting the end of the world, these same people couldn't even predict their own cultural extinction. And the reason why is because once again, just like with Nostradamus, they too used occult practices to get their information from.

It is well documented that the Mayans got their supposed prophetic information from the occult. They too were also involved in astrology and used hallucinogenic drugs that supposedly help them to speak to their dead ancestors, which is called necromancy. And their culture was extremely barbaric. They practiced human sacrifice, auto-sacrifice and used the blood of humans to 'appease the gods' because they believed the sun was powered by human blood.

And I'm supposed to listen to them over what God says in the Bible? I don't know about you, but come on, I think I'll stick to the tried and true Word of God in the Bible that was written over 1,500-years by 40 different authors over 40 generations that never once contradicts itself, has the same message through and through, and shows it had to come from God, over guys who practiced witchcraft, knew they were going to hell, did drugs and killed people including themselves just to keep the sun going! And yet, listen to this. "4% of Christians and 3% of non-Christians said they had consulted a medium or spiritual advisor within the past month." More Christians are seeking guidance from a demonic psychic than non-Christians do! And yet, not so surprisingly, just like with Nostradamus and the Mayans, they too are a faulty source of information.

Amid hundreds of prophecies, Biblical prophets are not known to have made a single error. However, a study of the prophecies made by psychics showed that of 72 predictions, only 6 were fulfilled in any way. However, 2 of these were vague and 2 others were hardly surprising, one of them being that the U.S. and Russia would remain leading world powers. Another study of the top 25 psychics and 72 of their predictions revealed that 92% were totally wrong. And the remaining 8 percent could easily be explained by chance and general knowledge of circumstances. In fact, in 1993 the psychics missed every single unexpected news story like Michael Jordan's retirement and the flooding in the Midwest. And among some of their false prophecies that year were that Kathy Lee Gifford would replace Jay Leno as host of *The Tonight Show* and the Queen of England would become a nun.

Okay, apparently, they forgot to tell her that. But here's the point. When in the world are we ever going to learn that those sources are not only, *not* a good source of truth, but this is why God tells us over and over again in the Bible that it really did come from Him. Just stick to it! Why? Because He doesn't want us lied to. He wants us to know the truth! And He wants us to know that these worldly false prophets are leading people astray!

The **2nd faulty source of truth** that people turn to instead of the Bible is what I call **Churchy False Prophets,** i.e. false prophets in the Church. But shocker, again, God says don't listen to these guys either! You're going to be deceived! But again, don't take my word for it. Let's listen to His!

Deuteronomy 18:20-22 "But a prophet who presumes to speak in My name anything I have not commanded him to say, or a prophet who speaks in the name of other gods, must be put to death." You may say to yourselves, 'How can we know when a message has not been spoken by the LORD?' "If what a prophet proclaims in the name of the LORD does not take place or come true, that is a message that the LORD has not spoken. That prophet has spoken presumptuously. Do not be afraid of him."

Why? Because he's a liar. What he said was from God was not from God because it's a lie! God doesn't lie! And so, here's the point. What are you supposed to do with that guy? According to the Old Testament, you were supposed to put that man to death! Or as other texts say, you are to stone them! But here's the point. Why do you put these guys to death? Because again, God's not a liar like us, He's Holy and He wants us to know the truth. So, if somebody has the audacity to say they're speaking for God and yet it turns out to be a lie, they die! Why? How dare you impugn the Holy character of God, right? And the good news is that today under the New Covenant we don't put a false prophet to death, but we are called to put them out of the Church! And yet, herein lies the problem. People today in the Church refuse to do this and so we're looking like a bunch of goobers. We're acting like God doesn't know what He's saying! And let me give you just a few examples of false prophets in the Church. Even though the Bible clearly says referring to the Second Coming of Jesus.

Matthew 24:36 "No one knows about that day or hour, not even the angels in heaven, nor the Son, but only the Father."

Harold Camping: He thinks he is smarter than God. He not only falsely predicted that the world would end on September 6, 1994, and that didn't happen, but again on May 21, 2011, and that didn't happen and then again on October 21, 2011 and he got that one wrong as well. Why? Because not even Harold Camping's mathematics can supersede God's Word. Nobody knows the day nor the hour, including Mr. Camping, I don't care how nifty he was with a calculator. In fact, he even stated that no one was saved between 1988 through 1994, and the Church Age ended in 1994, and that the Holy Spirit is no longer working in the Church. Sounds to me like the Holy Spirit was not working in Mr. Camping! Why? Because he's a false teacher making false predictions in the Church. And because of this many people to lose not only millions and millions of dollars, but several people even lost their lives. Why? Because the Church refused do what God said to do with false prophets. He should've been kicked out of the Church back in 1994 when he made his *first* false prediction! But that's not all. So is Benny Hinn. He's not only a false teacher ripping people off of their cash in the Church in the last days, just like the Bible said would happen, but he himself has made several false predictions himself. Here's the actual transcription.

Benny Hinn's False Prophecies

Benn Hinn: The Lord also tells me to tell you that in the mid 90's--about 94 or 95 no later than that. God will destroy the homosexual community from America. He will not destroy it with what many minds have thought it to be. It will start with fire. The Spirit tells me Fidel Castro will die in the 90's. Oh my, some will try to kill him, and they will not succeed, but there will come a change in his physical health and he will not stay in power and Cuba will be vigilant of God.

You know a prophetess has sent me a word to my wife right here and she said, "Tell your husband that Jesus is going to physically appear in his meetings. He may very well come back with footage of Jesus on the platform."

You know the Lord appeared in Romania recently. Now hear this. I'm prophesying this. Jesus Christ, the Son of God is about to appear physically in some churches and some meetings and to many of his people for one reason to tell you he's about to show up.[3]

So, let me get this straight. Jesus is about to show up to tell you he's about to show up. That's pretty amazing. You said God told you to tell us that the homosexual community would be destroyed by fire in the mid 90's and that didn't happen, and that Fidel Castro will die in the 90's and that didn't happen, and that Jesus appeared physically at your meetings and in other places around the world which is a contradiction to Scripture because it says Jesus only has two comings not three or four and I'm supposed to listen to you over God's Word in the Bible? According to God's Word, what should happen to Mr. Hinn? He should be kicked out of the Church! He's a liar and a false teacher and a false prophet! And he's leading people astray. Because we don't do that year after year it defames the authority of the Scripture. But he's not the only one. Another false prophet is Pat Robertson. He not only ran for President of the United States in the 1980's, but he even falsely prophesied who was going to be the President of the United States. Did he get it right? I don't think so! Check it out for yourself.

Benny Hinn/Pat Robertson: False Election Prophecy

Benny Hinn: I want to ask Pat about the coming election.

Pat Robertson: Mmm Hmm.

Hinn: What's your opinion on Obama, Romney. What happens if Obama wins. What happens if Romney wins and I'm talking about economy plus foreign policy.

Robertson: Well, he's not gonna have a second term. He's gonna win. Romney's going to win.

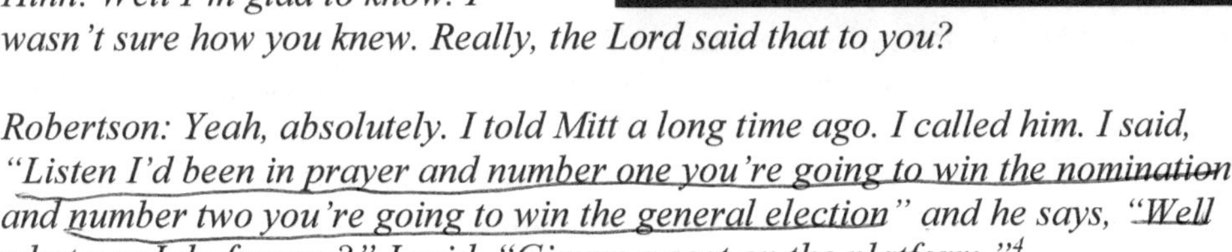

Hinn: You believe that?

Robertson: I absolutely believe that.

Hinn: What makes you believe that?

Robertson: Because the Lord told me. (Laughs)

Hinn: Well I'm glad to know. I wasn't sure how you knew. Really, the Lord said that to you?

Robertson: Yeah, absolutely. I told Mitt a long time ago. I called him. I said, "Listen I'd been in prayer and number one you're going to win the nomination and number two you're going to win the general election" and he says, "Well what can I do for you?" I said, "Gimme a seat on the platform."[4]

Real funny! And we wonder why the world laughs and mocks and scoffs at us? When we say that we know that this really came from God. And these guys, even in the church, year after year, and we let them remain. Letting them say God said this God said that. I'm telling you, if we want to avoid this embarrassment and hypocrisy, then we need to do what God tells us to do. Kick these false prophets and teachers out of the Church! Why? Because they're making God out to be a liar. If we would just stick to the Word of God in the Bible that was written over 1500-years by 40 different authors over 40 generations and never once contradicts itself and stop trying to seek a so called "word from God" outside the Word of God, then I'd say we'd have a better witness and we'd be better off! And therefore, you can't have it both ways. You can't agree with some of the Bible's teaching and then turn around and deny its authenticity. Why? Because the Bible clearly presents itself as the genuine Word of God. Anything short of this is intellectual hypocrisy. And so, it is with the skeptics of the Bible! They spout off bold claims that the Bible cannot be trusted, that the Bible is full of errors, yet all the time it is they who refuse to look at the evidence. So, I ask you, who's being the real hypocrite here? And this is why the last thing we'd ever want to do as a Christian, especially in these times when people are seeking the truth, is to treat the Bible like this guy.

Sunday 12:17pm:
Man enters apartment after Church services and places Bible on the table.
Monday: Bible still there
Tuesday: Still there
Wednesday: Still there
Thursday: Still there
Friday: Still there
Saturday: Still there
Sunday morning: Man grabs Bible where he left it last Sunday, almost as an afterthought, to head off for Church services.

I don't know about you, but that's got to be the ultimate hypocritical Christians behavior. And it's ironic that it's occurring at a time when people are in a desperate search for truth, that here we are as Christians saying; Oh yeah, the Bible really came from God, and you need to read it, it has all the answers you're looking for and yet, it's sitting on our kitchen tables just like everybody else's collecting dust. We have got to wake up and realize the golden opportunity God is giving us. Our world is in a frantic search for purpose and direction in life. People are full of questions like, "Why do I exist? Where did I come from? Why is all this evil going on? Is there life after death?" And how sad and ironic it is that this "mysterious" book that everyone's in search of can be found on bookshelves collecting dust in virtually every home in America, even in the Church. But be encouraged today. Let's get back on track. Let's not just say the Bible came from God, let's show the world the Bible really did come from God! Be encouraged today! You don't have to give into the attacks of the skeptic. You don't have to give into doubt. And you don't have to give in to one bit of criticism. What we hold in our hands is the genuine Word of God! Let's get busy reading it, studying it, applying it, and sharing it.

Chapter Two

Jesus & the Apostles Say So

How many of you would say that when you come to a church service, if nothing else you at least should get some good advice for living life. Right? That's at least bare, bare minimum. And that's why, I care about you, and I have to earn that paycheck, I'm here to help you out. I'm going to share with you some great advice for living life. Isn't that exciting? And it's not from me but from people that are much smarter than I. I'm going to share some great advice from kids. They are going to tell us how to have a great loving relationship. Isn't that a great way to start this year off? Let's take a look at what they have to say.

Practical Advice from Kids

What would you do on a first date that was turning sour?

(Craig, age 9) "I'd run home and play dead. The next day I would call all the newspapers and make sure they wrote about me in all the dead columns."

What is the proper age to get married?

(Tom, age 10) "Once I'm done with kindergarten, I'm going to find me a wife."

How do you decide whom to marry?

(Alan, age 10) "You got to find someone who likes the same stuff. Like, if you like sports, she should like it that you like sports, and she should keep the chips and dip coming."

How can a stranger tell if two people are married?

(Derrick, age 8) "You might have to guess, based on whether they seem to be yelling at the same kids."

When is it okay to kiss someone?

(Jim, age 10) "You should never kiss a girl unless you have enough bucks to buy her a big ring and her own DVD player, cause she'll want to have videos of the wedding."

Why do lovers often hold hands?

(Dave, age 8) "They want to make sure their rings don't fall off because they paid good money for them."

How do you make love endure?

(Randy, age8) "Be a good kisser. It might make your wife forget that you never take out the trash."

How would you make a marriage work?

(Ricky, age 10) "Tell your wife that she looks pretty even if she looks like a truck."

There's a lot of advice out there on living life. Probably the greatest advice I can give you as a pastor, not just in your relationship with your spouse, but in your relationship with God. Don't you ever, ever, ever, doubt that the Bible came from God. Last time you saw the unfortunate news, it doesn't matter Christian or non-Christian, they are starting to doubt the Bible came from God. It's due to a century or more of skepticism and false criticism towards the Bible and the hypocritical behavior of Christians and how they treat the Bible, they never even pick it up. That people, whether Christian or non-Christian are starting to doubt that the Bible really did come from God. So, to stave off this criticism and hypocrisy, even in the church, we are going to continue our study, *Did the Bible really come from God?* We are looking at 10 lines that of solid logical evidence that the Bible came from God. In the last chapter we saw that God tells us over and over that the Bible came from Him because he wants us to know the truth. The truth is what sets us free, not only in salvation but in sanctification and growing up in Christ. He is Holy, he doesn't lie like men. He wants us to know the truth and that's why he says the Bible came from him and you might want to read it once in a while. But he also says to stay away from the contrary, false worldly prophets and false churchy prophets. Because he says they are a bunch of liars that are out there to lead you astray and if they come near the church you need to kick them out. So, if you stay rooted in the Bible you will be just fine. You won't be discouraged or distracted.

The **2nd line of logical evidence** showing us that the Bible really did come from God is that **Jesus says so**. Now how many can say that if Jesus says something it's not only true, but He is the way, the truth, and the light. But again, don't take my word for it. Let's listen to His.

Matthew 4:1-11 "Then Jesus was led by the Spirit into the desert to be tempted by the devil. After fasting forty days and forty nights, He was hungry. The tempter came to Him and said, 'If you are the Son of God, tell these stones to become bread.' Jesus answered, 'It is written: Man does not live on bread alone, but on every word that comes from the mouth of God.' Then the devil took Him to the holy city and had Him stand on the highest point of the temple. 'If you are the Son of God,' he said, 'throw yourself down. For it is written: He will command His angels concerning you, and they will lift You up in their hands, so that You will not strike your foot against a stone.' Jesus answered him, 'It is also written: Do not put the Lord your God to the test.' Again, the devil took Him to a very high mountain and showed Him all the kingdoms of the world and their splendor. 'All this I will give you,' he said, 'if you will bow down and worship me.' Jesus said to him, 'Away from me, satan! For it is written: Worship the Lord your God and serve Him only.' Then the devil left Him, and angels came and attended Him."

So, here's the question. How do we know that the Bible really did come from God? What'd we just read? Jesus not only quoted the Scripture to combat satan himself, but He did so because He obviously believed that it carried the

Ultimate Authority, and that's exactly what we saw. Even the devil has to obey what the Bible says. Why? Because it really did come from God! And believe it or not, that's just the tip of the iceberg of what Jesus taught about the Bible. Let's take a look at some others.

• Divine Authority – Matthew 4:4-10
• Indestructibility – Matthew 5:17-18
• Infallibility – John 10:35
• Ultimate Supremacy – Matthew 15:3,6
• Factual Inerrancy – Matthew 22:29
• Historical Reliability – Matthew 12:40
• Scientific Accuracy – Matthew 19:4-5

In other words, He believed in a literal Adam with a literal Eve in a literal Garden where the first woman literally ate the first man out of literal house and home. And apparently, if you haven't heard, that's what Adam got for trying to cut a deal with God. "One day Adam was moping around in the Garden of Eden, feeling very lonesome, and so God asked him, 'What's wrong Adam?' And Adam answered that he didn't have anyone to talk to. So, God said He was going to give him a companion, and that it would be a woman. He said that this woman would cook for you, wash your clothes, always agree with every decision you make. She will bear your offspring and never ask you to get up in the middle of the night with them. She will not nag and will always be the first to admit she was wrong in a disagreement. She will never have a headache and will freely give you love and compassion. Adam asked God, 'What will a woman like this cost?' God said, 'An arm and a leg.' Adam said, 'What can I get for a rib?' The rest is history."

Seriously, what we see in the Bible is that Jesus clearly believed in a literal Adam, and a literal Eve, with a literal Garden of Eden, that happened in a literal 24-hour period. Why? Because the Bible really came from God! That's what Jesus believed and that's what He taught! So, here's the point. If Jesus is the Son of God, then logically that means that the Bible has to be *the Word of*

God. Why? Because "The authority of Jesus confirms the authority of the Bible." Or as one guy puts it this way:

"If Jesus is the Son of God, then the Bible is the Word of God. Only if one rejects the divine authority of Christ can he consistently reject the divine authority of the Scripture. If Jesus is telling the truth, then it is true that the Bible is God's Word. And even if you wanted to say Jesus were merely a prophet, then the Bible still is confirmed to be the Word of God through His prophetic office."

In other words, you can't have it both ways. You can't agree with some of Jesus' teaching and then turn around and deny the authenticity of the Bible. Because Jesus clearly presented the Bible as the genuine Word of God and anything short of this is intellectual hypocrisy. And yet, this is exactly what the skeptics do. They not only deny the fact that Jesus clearly taught that the Bible really did come from God, but they even go so far as to denigrate Jesus and the other clear evidences that He was Who He said He was, i.e. the Son of God, and therefore you might want to listen to Him and what He says, including that the Bible came from God.

The **1st thing the skeptics try to denigrate** about Jesus is **The Historicity of Jesus.**

And here's what they do. They'll typically state something like this, "Oh well, come on! This is a bunch of baloney anyway! Jesus didn't even exist. He only appears in the Bible that men made up to brainwash people with," right? How many of you have heard that before? Uh huh! It's all over the place. So, let's put that charge to the test. If Jesus really existed, then yeah, you'd think we'd find some other evidence of Him existing outside the Bible, right? Well guess what? We do! It's all over the place! In fact, let me give you just a few of the examples that are out there.

The Roman historian Tacitus wrote: *"Nero fastened the guilt on a class hated for their abominations, called Christians by the populace. Christus, (Latin for Christ) from whom the name had its origin, suffered the extreme penalty during the reign of Tiberius at the hands of Pontius Pilatus, and a most mischievous superstition, thus checked for the moment, again broke out not only in Judea, the first source of the evil, but even in Rome."*

Pliny the Younger, a Roman governor of Asia Minor wrote in A.D. 112 for advice on how to conduct legal proceedings against those accused of being Christians*: "They were in the habit of meeting on a certain fixed day before it was light, when they sang in alternate verses a hymn to Christ, as to a god, and bound themselves by a solemn oath, not to any wicked deeds, but never to commit any fraud, theft or adultery, never to falsify their word, nor deny a trust when they should be called upon to deliver it up; after which it was their custom to separate, and then reassemble to partake of food."*

Josephus, a first century Jewish historian wrote about Jesus: *"About this time there lived Jesus, a wise man, if indeed one ought to call him a man. For he wrought surprising feats. He was the Christ. When Pilate condemned him to be crucified, those who had come to love him did not give up their affection for him. On the third day he appeared, restored to life, and the tribe of Christians has not disappeared even to this day."*

The Babylonian Talmud, a collection of Jewish rabbinical writings compiled between 70 A.D. onward states: *"On the eve of the Passover Yeshu ("Yeshu" is Hebrew for Jesus) was hanged. (Hanged is also a synonym for crucifixion) For forty days before the execution took place, a herald cried, "He is going forth to be stoned because he has practiced sorcery and enticed Israel to apostasy."*

Lucian of Samosata a second century Greek satirist said: *"The Christians worship a man to this day, the distinguished personage who introduced their novel rites, and was crucified on that account. It was impressed on them by their original lawgiver that they are all brothers, from the moment that they are converted, and deny the gods of Greece, and worship the crucified sage, and live after his laws."*

Suetonius another Roman Historian from A.D. 69-140 said this about the Christian persecution of Nero in A.D. 64: *"He banished from Rome all the Jews, who were continually making disturbances at the instigation of one Chrestus. Punishment was inflicted on the Christians, a class of men given to a new and mischievous superstition."*

Thallus another historian who lived in the middle of the first century A.D. wrote around 52 A.D. about the darkness that fell during the crucifixion of Jesus as was quoted later by Julius Africanus: *"On the whole world there pressed a most fearful darkness; and the rocks were rent by an earthquake, and many places in Judea and other districts were thrown down."*

A Multitude of Writers In fact, that's not all. There are at least 42 different authors that mention Jesus within 150 years of His life. Now contrast this to the only 10 authors that mention Tiberious Caesar within 150 years of his life, who was the Roman Emperor during Jesus' ministry, and yet nobody questions his historical existence! Why not? If you're going to question Jesus with His 42 authors, then why aren't you questioning that guy with his 10? You can't have it both ways! Jesus not only appears all over the Bible all over the place, but He appears all over the place outside the Bible! Why? Because He's historically real! Therefore, I think the point is obvious. If Jesus not only says He was the Son of God in the Bible, and He's real, and if even secular sources confirm His existence, then I'm kind of thinking, we might want to listen to what He says, how about you? Including the fact that the Bible came from God, right?

The **2nd thing the skeptics** try to denigrate about Jesus is **The Uniqueness of Jesus.**

Now, here's what's funny, and hypocritical at the same time. Although the skeptics will flat out deny and refuse to believe that Jesus was God in the flesh and that He's the Savior of all mankind, even though that's what we see in the Bible, they will nonetheless label Him as a "good teacher." How many of you have heard that before? You know, just like Buddha, Mohammed, or Confucius. How many of you have heard that one before? Yeah, it's all over the place too, isn't it? But the problem is this "good teacher" mentality is ridiculous when you actually read the Bible. And I say that because if you actually read the Bible you'll see that Jesus did not leave us with the option of Him being merely a good teacher. Either He was a liar, which isn't consistent with His character we see in the Bible, or some form of a lunatic, which again isn't consistent with His character, or He was indeed who He said He was, i.e. *Lord God*! That's what you get if you actually *read the Bible*. But nonetheless, let's meet the skeptic on their terms and see just what it is that made Jesus so unique and unlike those other guys, Moe Larry and Curly.

The **1st unique thing** we see about Jesus is that **He was a Miracle Worker.**

You tell me which one of those guys, Moe, Larry and Curly, I mean, Buddha, Mohammed, and Confucius, ever did stuff like this. Let's take a look.

- Water converted into wine
- Heals the nobleman's son
- The catch of fish
- Heals the demoniac
- Heals Peter's mother-in-law
- Cleanses the leper
- Heals the paralyzed man
- Healing of the immobile man
- Restoring the withered hand
- Restores the centurion's servant
- Raises the widow's son to life
- Stills the storm
- Throws demons out of two men
- Raises the daughter of Jairus from the dead
- Cures the woman with the issue of blood
- Restores two blind men to sight
- Walks upon Lake Galilee
- Heals the daughter of the Syro-Phoenician woman
- Feeds more than 4,000 people
- Restores the deaf-mute man
- Restores a blind man
- Heals the epileptic boy
- Pays the temple tax by getting money from a fish's mouth
- Restores ten lepers to wholeness
- Opens the eyes of a man born blind
- Raises Lazarus from the dead
- Heals the woman with the spirit of infirmity
- Cures a man with dropsy
- Restores sight to two blind men near Jericho
- Condemns a fig tree
- Heals the ear of Malchus
- The second catch of fish

Now folks, here's the point. Did Buddha ever do those miracles? No! Did Confucius even do those things? I don't think so! How about Mohammed? No! Then how in the world can you say they're all the same and that Jesus was just like those other guys! It's ludicrous! Jesus is totally unique!

The **2nd unique thing** we see about Jesus is that **He was God.**

John 20:26-28 "A week later His disciples were in the house again, and Thomas was with them. Though the doors were locked, Jesus came and stood among them and said, "Peace be with you!" Then he said to Thomas, "Put your finger here; see my hands. Reach out your hand and put it into my side. Stop doubting and believe." Thomas said to Him, "My Lord and my God!"

Now I think it's pretty obvious, but Thomas not only said Jesus was *Lord* but He's Who? He *God*, right? And so, here's the point. Is Buddha God? No! Is Confucius God? No! How about Mohammed? I don't think so! Then how can you say they're all the same as Jesus? That's crazy! He's totally unique!

The **3rd unique thing** we see about Jesus is that **He was the Creator.**

Colossians 1:15-16 "He is the image of the invisible God, the firstborn over all creation. For by Him all things were created: things in heaven and on earth, visible and invisible, whether thrones or powers or rulers or authorities; all things were created by Him and for Him."

That means Jesus! So once again, here's the point. Did Buddha create the world? No! How about Confucius? No! Or how about Mohammed? No! Then how can you say they're all the same as Jesus when He's *radically different* than all the rest! He is totally unique, unlike those other guys, Moe, Larry and Curly, and that's why one man said this:

"People often ask what was so unique about Jesus? I mean, He possessed no certificates or degrees. He never traveled farther than 150 miles from where He was born. He lived and moved among common people and He was not an author. He wrote no books. He composed no poems, He compiled no documents, and the only sentence He wrote was a single line in the sand, which disappeared the same day.

He never used a fountain pen or even a typewriter or even Microsoft Word, and we have no line or syllable from His hand and yet do you realize that more books have been written about Him and His Words than any other Man in history? Do you realize that He has affected the lives of more people than all the authors of all the ages put together, and that the story of His life has now been translated in over 2,500 different languages and is read every year by billions of people?

No one ever spoke like this Man. His discourses have become the theme of millions of addresses and His Words are simple and clear. In fact, today, His sayings are hammered into polished marble, chiseled into imperishable granite, wrought into enduring bronze, and fashioned onto stained glass windows. His Words are literary gems. He stands today unequalled over all of literature. Shakespeare, Milton, Emerson, all bow their heads in His presence. Recognizing the Superior.

He was not a poet and yet He has inspired thousands of poets to honor their most sublime expressions. He was not a musician and yet He inspired Mozart, Shubert, Beethoven, Mendelson, Handel and the list goes on and on. He was not an artist, sculptor or painter yet He was the inspiration for Rafael, Michaelangeo, Leonardo DaVinci, Hoffman, and so many more.

He was not a doctor and yet He healed the sick, opened blind eyes, unstopped deaf ears, and He even raised the dead. He was not a statesman and never held nor aspired to a position, but He founded a Kingdom and He became the Conqueror of the world. And in just three short years of Christ's ministry here on earth, it has done more to

regenerate mankind than any other influence that has ever been felt in the history of mankind.

And that's why it remains true to this day that no single word grips the hearts of men like the blessed name of Jesus Christ. There's just something about that Name."[1]

Why? Because He's real, he really existed, not just in the Bible, but in history as well. Therefore, I'm kind of thinking that you might want to pay attention to what he said including what he said about the Bible.

The **3rd line of evidence** showing us that the Bible really did come from God is that the **Apostles say so.**

And this is yet another very important factor because although we may not know everything about the Apostles, we can deduce some things about them and what they experienced from the Bible. Since the Apostles experienced an amazing unity wherever they went, when you actually *read the Bible* it's very obvious that the Apostles truly believed that the Bible came from God, including what they were writing down for us, which was to become the New Testament. But don't take my word for it. Let's listen to theirs.

2 Peter 1:16,18,19,20-21 "We did not follow cleverly invented stories when we told you about the power and coming of our Lord Jesus Christ, but we were eyewitnesses of His majesty. We ourselves heard this voice that came from heaven when we were with Him on the sacred mountain. And we have the word of the prophets made more certain, and you will do well to pay attention to it. Above all, you must understand that no prophecy of Scripture came about by the prophet's own interpretation. For prophecy never had its origin in the will of man, but men spoke from God as they were carried along by the Holy Spirit."

So here we see that the Apostles did not just whoop up some book like the skeptics want to say, but they were actual eyewitnesses of God. And when they went about to record this account for us, it was guided along by the Holy Spirit, right? In fact, the Greek word there for "carried along" spoke of a ship that was being "driven" or "carried along" by the wind. And this is a picture of how true Biblical inspiration took place. Just as the men in a boat have the freedom to move around in the boat (their free will), even though the boat is actually being controlled by the wind, so it is with the process of Biblical inspiration. The writers of the Bible had the freedom to express their own personality and writing style, but the process was being watched over or "controlled" or "carried along" along by the "wind" if you will, of the Holy Spirit. This is true Biblical Inspiration. And this is *radically different* than other supposed sources of truth and their methods of inspiration. You tell me if it's not wise to stick to the Biblical method of inspiration.

Not like the Oracle of Delphi: For many centuries people went with this supposed source of prophetic truth and it all started one day when a goat herder noticed his sheep acting strange after they peered into a particular chasm.

It turns out that the chasm had a gaseous vapor that was being released from it and it caused the sheep to act "agitated" and become "frantic."

But soon they weren't the only ones. The next thing you know somebody actually set up a tripod over it, were these brain altering vapors from a crack in the ground, were now said to have caused a divine source of inspiration and thus you have the birth of the so-called prophet or Oracle of Delphi.[2]

Not like Automatic Writing: This is the occult process by which a writer, is taken over by a spirit, who then causes the writer to write down words on a piece of paper, without the use of their will, that the writer is clueless to.

Not like Channeling Messages: This is what we saw before where a person is not just taken over by another spirit to write down words on paper, but they actually take over their voice box and speak through them like these people.

"This man channels a spirit calling itself "Bashar" who seems to hold his audience spellbound as he tells them they are equal to the

Creator of the Universe.

"Bashar": That's why all are made in the image of the infinite Creator and what that means is you are all infinite creators.[3]

Jack Purcell has become one of the more popular channels possessed by a spirit named "Lazaris."

"Lazaris": Indeed, it a pleasure to be talking with you and uh well, shall we begin where you'd like to begin. Lazaris tells the listener that God is already within man and that if man wants to find God he only needs to find himself.[3]

Jane Roberts was a new age pioneer who channeled a spirit known as "Seth". Roberts sold more than a million copies of her books and have inspired many.

***Rick Stack:** Clearly the main message that Seth is trying to say is that people are gods in training. Some may find it interesting that the name Seth is synonymous with the Egyptian god Set. And in the realm of the occult, Set is one of the infernal names of satan."*[4]

Now that shouldn't be surprising to you because these people are full blown demon possession. But mention the occult and it's not all that different than Mormonism.

Not like Mormonism: Believe it or not, it is well documented that Joseph Smith used occult techniques to get his "new and improved" supposed revelation of Jesus Christ. Check this out.

Joseph Smith was a sorcerer and practiced crystal ball gazing or fortune telling and was convicted of this practice by the New York courts.

Smith's practice of magic and necromancy led him annually to a witchcraft holy day to the Hill Camora in New York, specifically to seek encounters with a spirit being called Moroni. During this time, he would attempt to conjure up the spirit from the dead.

There was strong evidence in 1824, Joseph Smith actually had to dig up the body of his dead brother Alvin and bring part of that body with him to the Hill Camora in order to gain access to the "gold" plates on which were written the Book of Mormon. It was also known within his community that Joseph Smith used blood sacrifices in his magic rituals to find hidden treasure.[5]

***C.R. Stafford** writes, "Joe Smith, the prophet, told my uncle William Stafford he wanted a fat black sheep. He said he wanted to cut its throat and make it walk in a circle 3 times around." After his death, Smith was found to be carrying a "magic" talisman on his person "sacred" to Jupiter, designed to bring him wealth, power and success in seducing women.*

Bill-former satanist and Mormon: "Behind me is the Los Angeles temple of the Mormon church and inside are many devout Mormons who are fulfilling what they consider to be godly, noble obligations to their faith and to their god. What they don't realize though, is that the rituals and the ceremonies that they are involved in are straight out of the occult.

How do I know that? Because I was a Mormon who went to the temple. I went to the temple many times, but more importantly I was also a high priest of satan. Before I joined the Mormon church I had 12 years of experience in witchcraft and satanism and when I went to the temple I was astounded at the high level of similarity the handshakes and the grips involved, the secret tokens of the Aaronic priesthood and the Melchizedek priesthood are in fact right out of witchcraft and satanism. The concept of putting on, as part of your priesthood robes, an apron which God rejected in the garden of Eden.

Lucifer himself in the temple says, 'This apron is a symbol of my power and priesthoods.' So, when I went through the temple I was ultimately very satisfied by it because I thought this was in fact, a profound satanic initiation ceremony.

All throughout the temple grounds here in Salt Lake City you will find all sorts of cult symbols.

Moloch
Symbol on Mormon Temple

Symbols that are generally associated with witchcraft and satanism. They are predominantly on the temples, but they are on such buildings as the Assembly Halls, and you can even find them in the visitor's center. I mean the place is virtually a Disneyland of occult symbols and yet there is absolutely no Christian symbol anywhere in here."[6]

Hmmm. I wonder why? Maybe it has to do with their method of so called inspiration? I don't know about you but I'm thinking I'm just going to stick to the Biblical method of inspiration over those guys who were involved in the occult, infested with demons, and sucked up gas to get a so-called a vision, how about you? But that's not all. So much so were the Apostles convinced that what they were writing really was from God, not gas or demons, or the occult, that they even said their writings were to be considered from God and included in the Bible.

2 Peter 3:15-16 "Bear in mind that our Lord's patience means salvation, just as our dear brother Paul also wrote you with the wisdom that God gave him. He writes the same way in all his letters, speaking in them of these matters. His letters contain some things that are hard to understand, which ignorant and unstable people distort, as they do the other Scriptures, to their own destruction."

Did you catch it? The Apostle Peter in their lifetime, actually called the Apostle Paul's writings *Scripture*! And for those of you who don't know, the word "Scripture" here is actually a "technical term" that was used to speak of "specialized writings" that carry the "authority of God" and were considered to be the actual "Word of God." And that's not the only one. Paul even quoted from the Gospel of Luke and he too places it on the rest of "Scripture" in 1 Timothy 5:18, so *logically* if Paul and Luke's writings were to be considered as Sacred writings that needed to be added to the Bible, then logically the other Apostles that were writing for us should be considered Sacred Scripture as well, right? They said so even in their own lifetime. In fact, so much so were the Apostles convinced of this, that what they wrote really did come from God, they not only said so, but we have the harsh warning in the last book of the Bible by the Apostle John, that no one should ever even dare tamper with the words they recorded for us in the Bible.

Revelation 22:18-19 "I warn everyone who hears the words of the prophecy of this book: If anyone adds anything to them, God will add to him the plagues described in this book. And if anyone takes words away from this book of prophecy, God will take away from him his share in the tree of life and in the holy city, which are described in this book."

In other words, don't touch it! I'd say the Apostles *seriously believed* that what they were writing really did come from God and you better not mess with it, how about you? And what you need to realize is that this warning is not applicable to just the Book of Revelation as some people would say. That's ludicrous! Think about it! If it only applied to the Book of Revelation alone, which is a part of the Bible, then does that mean you can go ahead and manipulate and mess up the rest of the Bible? That's crazy! Or, could it be that since the Book of Revelation is just one of the 66 books of the *whole* Bible and it just so happens to be at the *end* of the Bible, then maybe it applies to *all* of the Bible! Don't touch it! Why? Because it really came from God and that was what the Apostles believed. They believed that the Old Testament and the New Testament that they were writing really did come from God and they were willing to seal this belief with their lives. Everyone except John died a horrible death. Let's take a look at what happened to the Apostles.

- James, brother of John, was beheaded.
- Thomas was run through the body with a lance.
- Simon, brother of Jude, was crucified in Egypt.
- Simon the Zealot was crucified.
- Mark was burned and buried after being dragged through the streets.
- Bartholomew was beaten, skinned alive, crucified, then beheaded.
- Andrew was crucified.

- Matthew was killed by a spear.
- Philip was stoned and then crucified.
- James was thrown off the Temple and then clubbed to death.
- Peter was crucified upside down.
- Paul was beheaded.
- Luke was hanged upon an olive tree.
- Jude was shot to death by arrows.
- Matthias was first stoned then beheaded.
- Barnabas was stoned to death.
- John was put into a cauldron of boiling oil but survived and later died a ‘natural’ death.

If the Bible really were a lie, do you really think that every one of those Apostles would die a horrible death like that? I mean, you’d think if it really was a lie, that somewhere, somewhere along the line, at least one of them would’ve cracked and said something like this, “Okay, you got me? I was just kidding! Sorry about that! Whatever you do, don’t crucify me, don’t drag me through the streets, and please, don’t chop my head off or skin me alive, it was a lie.” But that’s not what we see! Every single one of them died a horrible death, save John who was tortured by the way. Why? Because they really believed that the Bible, including what they were writing for us, came from God! And contrast this to Joseph Smith, who although the Mormons would love to make him out to be a hero or some sort of a martyr like the true Apostles, he’s not! When called upon to stand up for his supposed “new” new testament, the Book of Mormon, he was fleeing like a coward running for his life! He was shot and killed by a mob of about 200 men for sleeping with their wives. And he was shot in the back twice while trying to jump out of a window! And they shot him one more time on the ground. He didn’t take it, he didn’t defend his source of truth. Running like a coward. And yet, we see every one of the Apostles of the REAL New Testament stood the test. Why? Because what they wrote for us really did come from God! And this is why you can’t have it both ways. You can’t agree with some of the Apostle’s teaching and then turn around and deny the authenticity of the Bible. Why? Because the Apostles clearly believed the Bible as the genuine Word of God. And anything short of this is total hypocrisy. And so, it is with the skeptics of the Bible! They spout off bold claims that the Bible cannot be trusted, that the Bible is full of errors. Yet it is they who refuse to look at the evidence. People be encouraged today! You don’t have to give into the attacks of the skeptic. You don’t have to give into doubt. What we hold in our hands is the genuine Word of God! And that’s why, more than ever, we’ve got to wake up and realize the golden opportunity that God is giving us. Our world is in a frantic search for purpose and direction and meaning to life. People are full of questions like, "Why do I exist? Where did I come from? Where is all this evil coming from? Is there life after death? And is there any hope?" And its high time that we the Church get busy not just *saying* the Bible came from God but *showing* the world that it did come from God. Why? Because even if you have to read this Book with your toe, it's the source of truth that tells us how God is not only real, but He really can make beauty out of ashes with your life, like He did for this guy.

Nick Vujicic (A man with no arms and no legs):

"I gave my life to Jesus Christ when I read John 9 at age 15, where a man was coming through a village--and a man, this blind man from birth, Jesus saw him. People said, 'Why was this man born that way.' Jesus said he was done so that the works of God may be revealed through him. And 2 Timothy 3:16 it says: 'All scripture is God-breathed.' And I believed God breathed in me life and faith. This faith came over me, this peace came over me and I felt like God answered my question."

Interviewer: *"And what was the question and what was the answer?"*

Nick: *"The question was 'Why? Why did you make me this way?' And the answer was: 'Do you trust Me?' That's the question, and when you say 'yes' to that question nothing else matters."*

Reporter: And it was in Jesus Christ where Nick found the strength what many thought would be the impossible.

(Video shows Nick waking up, turning lights on by himself. Shaving by himself. Using the computer. Climbing stairs. Doing many things without any help. Jumping in and swimming in the pool.)

Nick: *"And I thank God that He didn't answer my prayer when I was begging Him for arms and legs at age 8. Because guess what? Because I have no arms and legs, He is using me all around the world and we've seen so far, approximately-and this is conservative-200,000 souls come to Jesus Christ for the very first time in the last 6 or 7 years. And what would you rather, would you rather have arms and legs-no. What ever His will is, because I would rather have no arms and no legs temporarily here on earth. To be able to reach someone else for Jesus Christ."*[8]

He read the Bible with his *toe*, or what little he had left, and what happened? He found out that God really can make beauty out of ashes, no matter what! That's what our world needs to see, if we'd only read it with our hands as well.

Chapter Three

History & Transmission Say So

Well, I don't know about you, but wasn't it kind of a relief to finally graduate from high school? Were you like me, I finally get out of high school and I can finally just sit back and relax and enjoy life. No more having to crack the books. Did anybody else think that before me? But no, I found out that the learning process continues. At first, I was kind of bummed out about it. But then I found that there are a lot of important things that you can learn, believe it or, after high school. So much so, I have learned a massive number of important things after leaving. So important that I have to share it with you, are you ready? These are very important lessons in life.

Important Things in Life

- Never lick a steak knife
- If you ever find yourself behind another car in the Drive-Thru ATM where the person is actually using the Braille keypad on machine there…run!
- You can tell a man that there are 400 billion stars and he'll believe you, but if you tell him a bench has wet paint, he has to touch it.
- A plastic surgeon's office is the only place where no one gets offended when you pick your nose?
- When people apply deodorant, they will always have to use the exact same number of swipes under each arm.
- People will never answer the phone on the first ring. They will always wait until the second ring.

• The number of people watching you is directly proportionate to the stupidity of your action.
• Marriage is a relationship in which one person is always right and the other is a husband.
• People who keep running over a string a dozen times with their vacuum cleaner, then reach down, pick it up, examine it, then put it down o give their vacuum one more chance, these people need help.
• Never under any circumstances take a sleeping pill and a laxative on the same night.

As you can see there are a lot of important things in life you can learn. If you could have asked me, one of the most important things that people all around the world, including Christians, should learn is this, to never ever doubt that the Bible really came from God. And the reason I say that is that this is no longer the case in our world, even in the church. Christian, non-Christian, it doesn't matter, due to a century or more of skepticism and false criticism towards the Bible and unfortunately hypocritical behavior of the Christians and how they treat the Bible, they never pick it up. Christians, even in the church, are starting to doubt that the Bible did come from God. Therefore, to stave off this criticism we are going to continue our study, *Did the Bible really come from God?*

The **4th line of logical evidence** showing us that the Bible really did come from God is that **History says so.** But don't take my word for it. Let's listen to God's.

1 Corinthians 10:1-11 "For I do not want you to be ignorant of the fact, brothers, that our forefathers were all under the cloud and that they all passed through the sea. They were all baptized into Moses in the cloud and in the sea. They all ate the same spiritual food and drank the same spiritual drink; for they drank from the spiritual rock that accompanied them, and that rock was Christ. Nevertheless, God was not pleased with most of them; their bodies were scattered over the desert. Now these things occurred as examples to keep us from setting our hearts on evil things as they did. Do not be idolaters, as some of them were; as it is written: "The people sat down to eat and drink and got up to indulge in pagan revelry." We should not commit sexual immorality, as some of them did – and in one day twenty-three thousand of them died. We should not test the Lord, as some of them did – and were killed by snakes. And do not grumble, as some of them did – and were killed by the destroying angel. These things happened to them as examples and were written down as warnings for us, on whom the fulfillment of the ages has come."

So how do we know that the Bible really did come from God? Well, what did we just read? Apparently the 4th line of evidence is that History says so. What'd we just read? Paul not only said that the Old Testament history was written down for us, even today, as examples so we wouldn't do what they did, i.e. to sin against God, but here's the point. This admonition to pay attention to Old Testament and the New Testament history, i.e. the Bible, has been pretty much commonplace all throughout man's history. Why? Because the bulk of history believed that the Bible really did come from God, and you might want to listen to it! It's only been in recent years that people have become skeptical due to a century or more of false criticism and skepticism. But don't take my word for it. Let's listen to history.

The **1st proof that history believed** that the Bible really did come from God is shown by **Their Citations of it.**

Let's take a look at a list of just a few of our early history's citations of just the New Testament and you tell me if they didn't think it really did come from God.

- Justin Martyr - 330
- Hippolytus - 1,378
- Irenaeus - 1,819
- Clement Alex. - 2,406
- Eusebius - 5,176
- Tertullian - 7,258
- Origen - 17,922
- Grand Total - 36,289

You might think, "Well, whip dee do dah. So, what! What's the big deal about those guys quoting the New Testament so many times?" Well, here's the point. Stop and think about it. Why would they quote it so often, as a source of truth and authority, unless they *really believed* it came from God, who holds the Ultimate Authority? And besides, the effects of quoting the New Testament so many times has produced an interesting side-effect. Check this out.

Sir David Dalrymple was wondering about the dominance of Scripture in early writing when someone asked him, "Suppose that the New Testament had been destroyed, and every copy of it lost by the end of the third century, could it have been collected together again from the writings of the Early Church Fathers of the second and third centuries"' And after a great deal of investigation

Dalrymple concluded: "That question roused my curiosity, and as I possessed all the existing works of the Fathers of the second and third centuries, I commenced to search, and up to this time I have found the entire New Testament, except eleven verses." [1]

Now this is the point, this is the amazing truth. Even if the entire New Testament was completely destroyed, we could still reconstruct it *just from the quotations taken from early history*! The Bible is the only book in on the planet you can do this with. History clearly believed it came from God! And this early history witness is important, because just like in a crime scene investigation, you want the best, the earliest, and the most firsthand eye-witness accounts of people who were right on the scene when it happened, right? Of course! Well, this is what we have with the early history accounts. These people were right there on the scene when the Biblical events were taking place and so what they have to say about it carries much more weight than the skeptics today who are 2,000 years removed, right? How accurate can you be discerning a car wreck 2,000 year later, right? Next to none! But what we see with our early history is that these guys clearly believed that the Bible came from God! And so, you might want to listen to them. They're the accurate witness! But that's not all.

The **2nd proof** that history believed that the Bible really did come from God is shown by **Their Canonicity of it.**

Or in other words, how the Bible came to be. And this is an important point because usually the skeptic will say something like this, "Well okay, fine. Maybe early history believed that the Bible came from God, but how do we know the books we have in the Bible today, are the actual ones that are supposed to be there? Haven't you heard? There's lost letters of the Bible that somebody's trying to hide from us?" How many of you have heard that before? Yeah, it's all over the place. And this is why it's important to understand the *canonicity*, or in other words, how the books of the Bible were chosen. When you look at the facts, you'll see there was absolutely no conspiracy at all! Rather, the Early Church was *extremely careful* to get it right. They actually put into place a logical filter to help discover which books had the mark of God and were logically qualified to be in the Bible. Let's take a look.

- Was the author of the book an Apostle?
- Does it agree with the rest of Scripture?
- Was it accepted by the Early Church?
- Was it circulated by the Early Church?
- Was it quoted by the Early Church?
- Did it come with the Power of God?

So, as you can see with this logical filter in place, the Early Church really didn't so much *determine* which books were to be in the Bible, as it was that they *discovered* which books were *already* qualified to be in the Bible. There's no secret conspiracy going on here, and neither is there anything willy nilly about them choosing which books were to be in the Bible. They were extremely careful and logical, and it was guided by God. In fact, the canon of the Scripture was pretty well set by 150 A.D., which is well before Constantine, and well before the first Church Council, and well before the first Pope and the birth of the Roman Catholic Church. And this is important because people out there want to say that these entities have secretly kept out certain books that should've been in there,

you know, those "lost books of the Bible," They're hiding it from us. Really? As we just saw, the canon of the Bible was pretty much set by 150 A.D. and the books that were rejected were rejected for good reason. They didn't make it through the logical filter. And yet, the whole reason why this "conspiracy theory idea" of the so-called "lost books" of the Bible is even experiencing a revival of sorts is because there's a book out there, that was even made into a movie called, "The DaVinci Code." How many of you have heard of that? But the problem is, once you look at the facts you see that Dan Brown, the author, was either a really, really bad researcher or a flat-out liar because he's full of errors and inconsistency. For instance, he said that Jesus had kids, was actually married and there are thousands of manuscripts proving this, that they're hiding from us. Really? Here's the actual conspiracy. Check out the facts!

Brian Edwards*: "You know it's quite amazing how scholars and others insist on propagating something that has absolutely no support. As an aside, take the popular idea that was popularized by Dan Brown in the DaVinci Code that Jesus married Mary Magdalene.*

There are even, and I read them, there are even academics who assume that. They take it up. Well let me tell you that there is not a single text in all the gnostic writings that we have to record that Jesus married Mary Magdalene. Not a single text and yet still, the myth is propagated."[2]

Did you catch that? Not a single text. In other words, his lie continues to spread. Why? Because he knows the axiom. If you repeat a lie loud enough, long enough, and often enough, people will believe it. Including in a book or a movie called, "The DaVinci Code." It's a lie! But you might be thinking, "Wait a second. Didn't they find in the news a fragment that said Jesus had a wife?" No. They found a *tiny fragment* with some writing on it. Does that mean it was part of the Bible? No. But let's say it was legit. The phrase they are picking up says, and I quote, "Jesus said to them, 'My wife…" and was cut off. So that's what they are basing it off of, a single piece of paper. First of all, how many times in the Scripture does Jesus refer to us the Church as His Bride or wife, right? So that means nothing. Second, they're guessing the fragment dates from the 4th century, long after the Gospels were written. They're just trying to tie it in. And third, even the secular researchers studying the fragment said, "this doesn't prove anything definitive about Jesus," and I quote, "*Faking antiquities is not uncommon*," which is why many people are already saying the fragment is yet another in a lengthy line of fakes trying to dupe people, like with the DaVinci Code!

It's a bunch of baloney and yet the press just runs with it! And so, it is with these so-called "lost books" of the Bible. When you look at the facts, you'll see they were never lost! They were rejected long ago, and for good reason! In fact, once you read them for yourselves you'll see they actually excluded themselves from the Bible! You don't even need to do it. It's self-evident!

Judas Gospel: was published for us in 2006, but it has been known ever since 180 A.D. where it was rejected. It made Judas Iscariot, the one who betrayed Jesus, out to be some sort of a hero.

Letter of Herod: The person writing this letter actually forged this letter and we know that because they actually forgot that the Herod mentioned at the time of Jesus' birth was not the same Herod at His trial and crucifixion.

Gospel of Thomas: It tries to give us secret details about Jesus' early years as a child and says amongst other wild things that, "As Jesus was playing, a child bumps into Him and Jesus strikes him dead."

Acts of John: which states that, "John comes into an inn and there are bedbugs in the bed and John commands the bedbugs to get out of the bed and they get out of the bed and march in a line out of the room."

Acts of Paul: which says, "Paul baptizes a lion and later this lion saved him in the amphitheater."

Protoevangelium of James: which was written to perpetuate the false teaching of the perpetual virginity of Mary and says that, "She was placed in the Temple at the age of three and that angels fed her."

Uh, yeah right! Somebody's got bed bugs alright! They've got bed bugs on the brain! But when you look at the facts it's crazy, they are trying to bait us. As you guys can see, these so-called lost books of the Bible were rubbish then and guess what? They're rubbish today. They weren't lost, they just keep trying to resurrect them to you and me. There is no conspiracy!

But some will still say, "Okay, maybe there weren't any lost books of the Bible, but what about those other books that people like the Catholics have in their Bible called the *Apocrypha*? Which means hidden writings. What about those? How come we don't have those? Well, first of all, the *Apocrypha* books didn't make it into the Protestant Bible for the same reasons why the other books didn't make it into the Bible. They never passed it through the logical filter, also the Jewish people never once quoted the *Apocrypha* in their Bible, Jesus and the Apostles never once quoted the *Apocrypha* in the Bible. AND the reason why the Catholic Church did this was to not only distinguish themselves from the Protestant Bible, but it was to also justify several of their false teachings, like praying for the dead and even purgatory, which appears nowhere in the Bible!

And for those of you who don't know, purgatory is the false teaching where the Catholic Church says when we die we go to some sort of "holding pen" where we purge our sins through fire and suffering so we can hopefully make it to heaven, if ever! Then you can pay the Catholic Church, even today. But if you know your Bible, that's not only ludicrous, it's blasphemous.

2 Corinthians 5:8 says, "Absent from the body, is to be present with the Lord." When we die, praise God, we go straight to be with Jesus! Not some holding pen to suffer for our sins! Purgatory is actually a slap in the face to the atonement of Christ, because it says that His sacrifice on the cross was not sufficient payment for all our sins. That's blasphemy! Besides, I don't know about you, but I don't think I want to trust anybody who can't even get *The Ten Commandments* right in their so-called Bible.

Here's our Ten Commandments.

1. You shall have no other gods before me.
2. You shall not make for yourself an idol in the form of anything.
3. You shall not misuse the name of the Lord your God.
4. Remember the Sabbath day by keeping it holy.
5. Honor your father and your mother.
6. You shall not murder.
7. You shall not commit adultery.
8. You shall not steal.
9. You shall not give false testimony against your neighbor.
10. You shall not covet.

Now here's the Catholic altered version.

1. You shall have no other gods.
2. You shall not take the Lord's name in vain.
3. Keep holy the Lord's day.
4. Honor your father and mother.
5. You shall not kill.

6. You shall not commit adultery.
7. You shall not steal.
8. You shall not bear false witness against your neighbor.
9. You shall not covet your neighbor's wife.
10. You shall not covet your neighbor's goods.

The Ten Commandments

Love God	Love Others
1. I am the LORD your God: You shall not have strange gods before me. 2. You shall not take the name of the LORD your God in vain. 3. Remember to keep holy the LORD'S Day.	4. Honor your father and your mother. 5. You shall not kill. 6. You shall not commit adultery. 7. You shall not steal. 8. You shall not bear false witness against your neighbor. 9. You shall not covet your neighbor's wife. 10. You shall not covet your neighbor's goods.

Now did you notice what was missing and added there? The second commandment was missing, "You shall not make for yourself an idol in the form of anything." Why? Why would they take it out? Because if you know anything about the Catholic Church, figurines and idol worship are big money and big religion. You need the figurines that you can buy so you can have them blessed by the Priest and pray to. Then they say keep the Lord's day, honor your father and mother and thou shalt not kill. Unfortunately, ours say murder and theirs say kill. Murder and kill are two different things. The New Agers and the animal activists will take that and say, 'See we shouldn't kill animals. We can't eat them.' Then it says you shall not commit adultery, shall not steal, and shall not bear false witness against your neighbor. But you still must have a list of "ten" Ten Commandments so they take the last commandment and split it into "two" to make it ten again! A complete mockery of Scripture. You shall not covet your neighbors' wife and you shall not covet your neighbor's goods. I don't know about you, but I'm not going to trust anything they have to say about the Bible.

I'll stick to the Early Church's canonicity of the Bible, how about you? Much more logical and reliable!

The **3rd proof** that history believed that the Bible really did come from God is shown by **Their Creeds of it.**

You tell me if history's greatest minds, rulers, and thinkers throughout all of history give glowing opinions about the Bible really coming from God. Let's take a look.

W.E. Gladstone: *"I have known ninety-five of the world's great men in my time, and of these eighty-seven were followers of the Bible."*

Napoleon: *"The Bible is no mere book, but a Living Creature, with a power that conquers all that oppose it."*

Queen Victoria: *"That book accounts for the supremacy of England."*

Immanuel Kant: *"The existence of the Bible, as a book for the people, is the greatest benefit which the human race has ever experienced. Every attempt to belittle it is a crime against humanity."*

Charles Dickens: *"The New Testament is the very best book that ever was or ever will be known in the world."*

Sir William Herschel: *"All human discoveries seem to be made only for the purpose of confirming more and more strongly the truths contained in the Sacred Scriptures."*

Sir Isaac Newton: *"There are more sure marks of authenticity in the Bible than in any profane history."*

Abraham Lincoln: *"I believe the Bible is the best gift God has ever given to man. All the good from the Savior of the world is communicated to us through this book."*

George Washington: *"It is impossible to rightly govern the world without God and the Bible."*

Daniel Webster: *"If there is anything in my thoughts or style to commend, the credit is due to my parents for instilling in me an early love of the Scriptures. If we abide by the principles taught in the Bible, our country will go on prospering and to prosper; but if we and our posterity neglect its instructions and authority, no man can tell how sudden a catastrophe may overwhelm us and bury all our glory in profound obscurity."*

W.H. Seward: *"The whole hope of human progress is suspended on the ever-growing influence of the Bible."*

Patrick Henry: *"The Bible is worth all other books which have ever been printed."*

U.S. Grant: "*The Bible is the sheet-anchor of our liberties."*

Horace Greeley: *"It is impossible to enslave mentally or socially a Bible reading people. The principles of the Bible are the groundwork of human freedom."*

Andrew Jackson: "*That book, sir, is the rock on which our republic rests."*

Robert E. Lee: *"In all my perplexities and distresses, the Bible has never failed to give me light and strength."*

John Quincy Adams: "*So great is my veneration for the Bible that the earlier my children begin to read it the more confident will be my hope that they will prove useful citizens of their country and respectable members of society. I have for many years made it a practice to read through the Bible once every year."*

It looks to me like the world's greatest minds, rulers, and thinkers throughout all of history really believed the Bible came from God, how about you? And if you put all this together, you'll see what's ludicrous. Those who doubt the authenticity of the Bible assume their doubting position has been commonplace throughout history. But as we just saw, nothing could be further from the truth. The belief that the Bible really came from God was virtually held by nearly everyone for the last 2,000 years of History…in the Church…outside of the Church. Therefore, one who doubts the authority of the Bible is forced to say that their own private knowledge of the Bible is greater then all the greatest thinkers and scholars of the Bible for the last 2,000 years, right? Now, this is *totally absurd* when one takes into account that most people who doubt the authority of the Bible have rarely, if ever, even read the Bible, let alone studied it! And yet, you speak with such authority? And this is why you can't have it both ways. You can't agree with some of history's teaching and what they document and then turn around and deny the authenticity of the Bible. Why? Because the bulk of man's history clearly presents the Bible as the genuine Word of God. And anything short of this is hypocrisy.

The **5th line of evidence** showing us that the Bible really did come from God is that **Transmission Standards say so.**

2 Peter 1:16,18,19,20-21 "We did not follow cleverly invented stories when we told you about the power and coming of our Lord Jesus Christ, but we were eyewitnesses of His majesty. We ourselves heard this voice that came from heaven when we were with Him on the sacred mountain. And we have the word of the prophets made more certain, and you will do well to pay attention to it. Above all, you must understand that no prophecy of Scripture came about by the prophet's own interpretation. For prophecy never had its origin in the will of man, but men spoke from God as they were carried along by the Holy Spirit."

Now this is the passage we saw before where Peter says he and the Apostles did not just whoop up some book like the skeptics want to say, but they were actual eyewitnesses of God and when they went about to preserve this eyewitness account for us, i.e. transmit it for us, it was guided along by the Who? By the Holy Spirit, by God, right? Yet, even when you share this with the skeptic, they still say something like this, "Well even if what was originally spoken to the people in the Bible really did come from God, there's no guarantee that what we have today is totally accurate." Really? And then they'll usually cite the typical scenario where people play the game of saying a phrase to one person in a circle who then whispers it to the next person in the circle and so on and so forth, and finally the last person in the circle shares what they heard and invariably the message is totally different from the original statement. Then they reply that this is proof of why the Bible could never have maintained its integrity. But those who make this ridiculous assumption are only showing their ignorance of how the Bible has been preserved for us throughout history. It has amazing transmission standards!

For instance, many people will look at the Old Testament, especially the first five books of the Bible, which were written by Moses and ask, "How in the world could Moses know what went on in the Genesis account, the Garden of

Eden, the flood, etc. when he is so far removed from the actual events? How can we trust what he wrote?" Well it's simple. That's why you need to pay attention to the genealogical record in the Book of Genesis. You know, that part in the Bible that most people skip over that says so and so begot so and so? Well, there's an interesting thing that happens when you do your homework. You see, if you add up the years and chart them out, you discover that the lifespan of many of those people overlap each other. The chart below tells us that Adam knew Methuselah for 243 years.

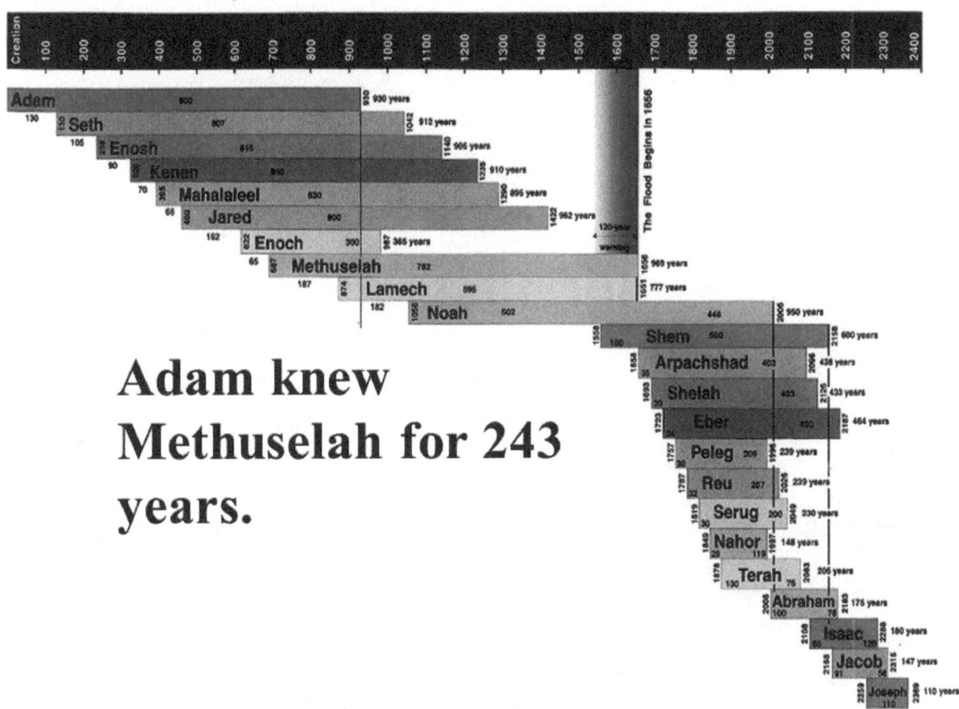

Methuselah was the one that said that when he died the flood was going to come. Wouldn't you say you could have several conversations with him during that 243 years? Methuselah knew Noah for 600 years. Noah had 6 living ancestors that could've personally known Adam. So, he could have got information not only from Methuselah but from several other guys. Noah was still alive 58 years after Abraham was born. Abraham could still have talked to Noah, a direct survivor of the flood. In fact, all 10 of Abraham's post-flood ancestors (even Noah) were still alive for his early life. And even more interesting is that Noah's son Shem was still alive not just for Abraham, but even Isaac and Jacob! A direct survivor of the flood if you add up the dates.

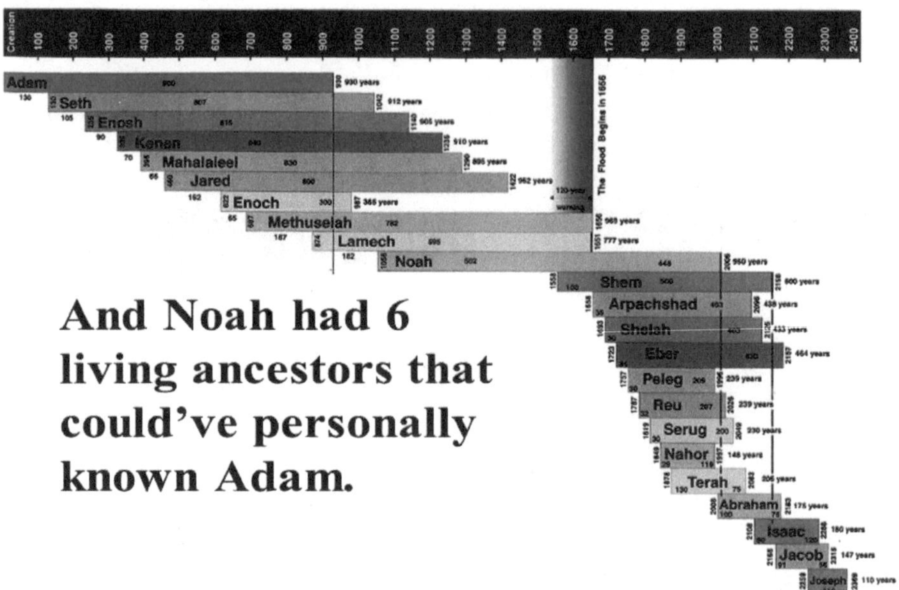

Thus, the first 2,157 years of mankind's history is covered by the lives of just 3 men! So much for talking around the circle trying to get it right.

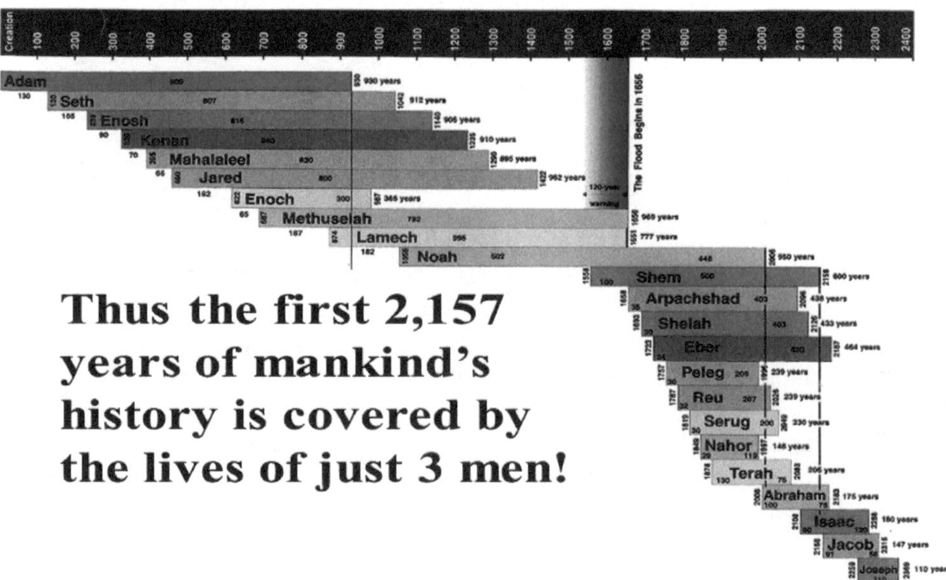

Moses did not just whoop up some story. The transmission of data from the beginning of man's history is not only possible accurately, but it could've been retrieved from firsthand accounts. Furthermore, we need to keep in mind that the authors of the Old Testament didn't just arbitrarily write down some message and hopefully somebody got it right, copied it, with no errors. No! If you study Jewish history, you'll see that they followed strict copying methods for the specific reason of having an accurate transmission of the data. Let me show you what I mean. There's nothing willy-nilly here!

• A synagogue roll must be written only by a Jewish person and on the skins of clean animals.

• The scrolls must be fastened together with strings taken from clean animals.

• Every skin must contain a certain number of lines and columns, equal throughout the entire codex.

• The ink should be black, neither red, green, nor any other color, and be prepared according to a definite recipe.

• No word or letter, not even a *yod*, can be written from memory. You must look at the codex before you.

• The copyist must sit in full Jewish dress, wash his whole body, not write the Name of God without a pen newly dipped in ink, and even if a king should address him while writing that Name, he must take no notice of him.

In fact, their manuscripts were checked within 30 days and even if it had one mistake, it was destroyed by burning it, and even the ashes were buried just to make sure no one would ever find the remains. Therefore, as you can see, this again, is a far cry from the common scenario of just "talking around a circle" don't you think? But what about the New Testament? Just how was it transmitted to us? Is what's recorded for us there reliable? Well let's take a look at some of the common practices of the student of a Rabbi, back in the days of Jesus. For instance, a good student back in those days was one who did not lose one drop of the rabbi's teaching. And the way they did that was by memorizing literally word for word what they were doing or taught. Also, a Rabbi back in those days would purposely teach in parables and other poetic forms making his teachings even easier to memorize. And guess what method of teaching *Rabbi Jesus* used? The exact same thing! Therefore, He purposely made it easy for His disciples to memorize all His teachings, so they would not lose a drop! But that's still not all. The Apostles also had the promise of Jesus' sending of the Holy Spirit to remind them of what He's taught them to ensure the accuracy of what they recorded down for us.

John 14:25-26 "All this I have spoken while still with you. But the Counselor, the Holy Spirit, whom the Father will send in My Name, will teach you all things and will remind you of everything I have said to you."

And what you've got to keep in mind is that these strict and reliable forms of transmission standards are unique to the Bible alone. Most of the books of antiquity that the skeptics assume are reliable don't even come close to following these kinds of standards, let alone have any, yet they believe they're true! In fact, let me give you some examples. For instance, how about the reliability of the so-called transmission standards of the Jehovah's Witnesses? Should we trust their version of the Bible? I don't think so but let's look at the facts. Let's see how they transmitted their version.

Jehovah's Witnesses and the New World Mistranslation

A former Jehovah's Witness: *"The bible produced by the Jehovah's Witness called "The New World Translation" has caused quite a stir. 'We are prepared to document that Charles Russell believed he was the sole channel of communication between God and men. He even referred to himself as God's mouthpiece.'*[3]

Lorri MacGregor: *"I was surprised to find out many strange things about Pastor Russell when I did independent research on him. Here, in "The Finished Mystery" book, he taught that the churches of Christendom were started by bald headed men with smoke on their brains. He thought that if a dog's head were shaped like a man's, the dog could think like a man. Johannes Greber was a former Roman Catholic priest and after getting married to a woman who was herself a medium, he got the idea that he could translate the New Testament in a more accurate way if he would have some help from a spirit medium. When the occult background of Greber was exposed by those outside the society, they stopped referring to him as a scholar. Interestingly the evidence is that they knew about his occult involvement for nearly 30 years. This kind of deliberate cover-up is found throughout their history."*[4]

Joan Cetnar (former headquarters member): *"My late husband Bill Cetnar was at the Watchtower headquarters during the work on the New World Translation. Former president Fred Franz was mainly responsible for the translation work. He was neither a Hebrew nor a Greek scholar and only had two years of college. There were no scholars. I know because I knew them all personally. The so-called translation was written to reflect their own peculiar doctrines. It's a sham kind of scholarship. This could be called, not a separate version of the bible, in this respect it's a perversion of the bible."*[5]

Dave Riccaboni (former headquarter's member): *"The only original Greek I knew was George Gangas of the secretive translation committee and he was no scholar that's for sure. Because he himself told me that before he came to Bethel, he was a short order cook in Columbus, Ohio."*[6]

I don't know about you but I'm kind of thinking I'm going to stick to our version of the Bible with it's strict and reliable transmission standards, over that one that was inspired by a guy involved in the occult, who believed in bald headed men with smoke coming off their brains, not to mention talking dogs, and was compiled by a short order cook and others who knew nothing about Biblical languages! But that's not all. Jehovah's witnesses go on to literally delete, chop out, and insert passages into the Bible that are not there just to prop up their false teachings to make them sound palatable. That's not an accurate transmission. But they're not the only ones. So are the Seventh Day Adventists. They do the exact same thing with their perversion of the Bible called the "Clear Word Bible." And the only thing "clear" about it is that it's not trustworthy at all. Don't believe me? Check it out for yourself!

Ellen G. White and Seventh Day Adventists

"During the mid-1800's within a few years of each other-Mormons, Jehovah's Witnesses, Christian Scientists and Seventh Day Adventists were all presenting doctrines contrary to those held by traditional Bible believers. The central Adventists doctrine, which states that the judgment of believers works will determine their salvation is blatantly unbiblical and is not taught by any legitimate Christian denomination.

Other heretical Adventist doctrines include the teaching that Christ's atonement for sins on the cross was incomplete, that Jesus Christ is Michael the Archangel and that there is no hell.

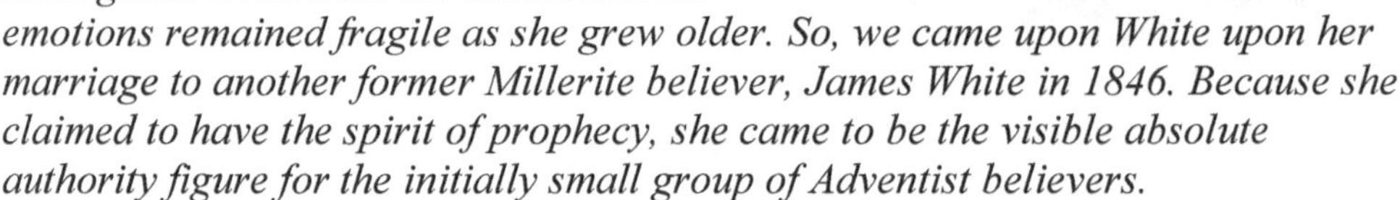

The late Seventh Day Adventist founder Ellen G. White, born on November 26, 1827 in Gorham, Maine. Ellen was hit in the head with a rock at the age of 9. She remained unconscious for three weeks.

Unable to attend school following the incident. Ellen's education ceased at the third-grade level. Both her health and her emotions remained fragile as she grew older. So, we came upon White upon her marriage to another former Millerite believer, James White in 1846. Because she claimed to have the spirit of prophecy, she came to be the visible absolute authority figure for the initially small group of Adventist believers.

Her writings grew to be seventeen times as large as the entire Bible. Her followers were to reference these 5,000 articles, 49 books, plus 55,000 manuscript pages she claimed to write and regard them as being as inspired as the Bible. They have, however, made her more embarrassing writings unavailable, locking them securely away in the White Estate vault. Mrs. White, in a vision, also claimed to have traveled complete with wings to various planets which were full of inhabitants.

She reported meeting Enoch on a distant planet during one of her journeys. Other times, she saw angels using golden gate passes to go in and out of heaven. Some of her so-called visions reflected her own racist views. For example, she believed certain races of people were the result of sexual relations between man and animal, which she referred to as an amalgamation.

Despite the unbiblical nature of her visions, her followers continued to accept her as God's messenger, and her writings as inspired as the Bible. They have their own version of the Bible known as the Clear Word Bible, which insert the words and ideas of Ellen G. White directly into the biblical text. One can see the extent to which Seventh Day Adventists are prepared to go to support their "prophetess" even to the manipulation of scripture."[7]

Now again, maybe it's just me, but I think I'll stick to our version of the Bible with it's strict and reliable transmission standards over that one, that what? Came from a false prophetess who denied orthodox Christian doctrine, taught false teachings, and believed that certain races today are a result of breeding done with animals, and then insert that into your so-called Bible! No thanks! I'll stick to ours! And therefore, you can't have it both ways. You can't accept some books of antiquity that have little or no standard of reliable transmission, like those, and then turn around and deny the authenticity of the Bible. Why? Because the Bible's unique, amazing, and reliable historical transmission standards clearly present it as the *genuine Word of God.* And anything short of this is called hypocrisy. And so, it is with the skeptics of the Bible! They spout off bold claims that the Bible cannot be trusted, that the Bible is full of errors. Yet it is they who refuse to look at the evidence. People be encouraged today! You don't have to give into the attacks of the skeptic. You don't have to give into doubt. You don't have to give into one iota of criticism! What we hold in our hands is the genuine Word of God! And that's why, more than ever, we've got to wake up and realize the golden opportunity that God is giving us. Our world is in a frantic search for purpose and direction and meaning to life. They realize the world is messed up and it's getting worse! And so, they're full of questions like, "Why do I exist? Where did I come from? Where is all this evil coming from? Is there life after death? And is there any hope?" And its high time that we the Church get busy not just saying the Bible came from God but showing the world that it really did come from God, and the way we do that is by treating it just as good as our cell phones. What if our Bible was just as important as our cell phone?

- *We treated it like we couldn't live without it.*
- *When we forgot it, we went back to get it.*
- *We had lots of gadgets to keep us connected to it.*
- *We always had it close by in case of an emergency.*
- *We carried it around in our purses and pockets.*
- *We checked it throughout the day for new messages.*
- *We were constantly going over our minutes every month.*
- *We made sure our battery never ran low.*
- *What if our Bible was just as important as our cell phone?*

What if? I think we'd not only experience revival ourselves, but I think our world would take us much more seriously when we tell them about Jesus, and His Words of Truth in the Bible, how about you? That's what our world needs to see. Let's be that kind of Church this year.

Chapter Four

Manuscripts & Archeology Say So

If you can remember in the last chapter I shared this little joke about marriage and it basically said this. Marriage is a relationship in which one person is always right and the other one is the husband. But to be honest with you I felt a little guilty about that, as a fellow man, and I want to make it up to you, right guys? We have to stick together so I am going to share with you the top 10 things that men know about women. Men are you ready to shine?

1.
2.
3.
4.
5.
6.
7.
8.
9.
10.

Well that just about does it. As you can see we men may not know a lot about you ladies but there is something that we do all know, whether you are men or women, that you do not need to doubt that the Bible really did come from God. But, as we have been seeing, unfortunately, that is no longer the case. Whether Christian or non-Christian it doesn't seem to matter.

The **6th line of logical evidence** showing us that the Bible really did come from God is that **Manuscripts Say So.** But don't take my word for it. Let's listen to God's.

Colossians 4:7-16 "Tychicus will tell you all the news about me. He is a dear brother, a faithful minister and fellow servant in the Lord. I am sending him to you for the express purpose that you may know about our circumstances and that he may encourage your hearts. He is coming with Onesimus, our faithful and dear brother, who is one of you. They will tell you everything that is happening here. My fellow prisoner Aristarchus sends you his greetings, as does Mark, the cousin of Barnabas. (You have received instructions about him; if he comes to you, welcome him.) Jesus, who is called Justus, also sends greetings. These are the only Jews among my fellow workers for the kingdom of God, and they have proved a comfort to me. Epaphras, who is one of you and a servant of Christ Jesus, sends greetings. He is always wrestling in prayer for you, that you may stand firm in all the will of God, mature and fully assured. I vouch for him that he is working hard for you and for those at Laodicea and Hierapolis. Our dear friend Luke, the doctor, and Demas send greetings. Give my greetings to the brothers at Laodicea, and to Nympha and the church in her house. After this letter has been read to you, see that it is also read in the church of the Laodiceans and that you in turn, read the letter from Laodicea."

So how do we know that the Bible really did come from God? Well, what did we just read? Apparently the 6th line of evidence is that *Manuscripts* or *Copies of the Letters of the Bible* say so. And this is apparently what the skeptics seem to miss. What'd we just read? Paul said to the Colossians that when they were done reading that letter that they got from Paul, that they should what? They should pass that letter on to the Church of Laodicea and then get busy reading that one that he wrote to them, right?

And here's the point. This massive number of letters, which eventually became the Bible, 27 in the New Testament and 39 in the Old, is a huge proof that the Bible really did come from God. And this is important to know because the skeptics will usually come back and say something like this, "Well even if the Bible was transmitted reliably by the authors of the Bible, we still can't be sure of the accuracy since we don't have the original copies." But nothing could be further from the truth. Why? Because the more manuscript copies of a document you have, the more you can cross-reference the copies to ensure that what you have is accurate to the original.

Sir Frederick Kenyon stated this: *"The last foundation for any doubt that the Scriptures have come down to us as they were written has now been removed."*

And this truth really hits home *especially* when you compare the manuscript copies of the Bible to other works of antiquity, whose validity is never questioned mind you. Let's look first at the New Testament. And as you'll soon see, the results are quite embarrassing, for the skeptic.

Author	When Written	Earliest Copy	Time Span	Copies
Homer (Iliad)	900 B.C.	400 B.C.	500 yrs.	643
Pliny	A.D. 61-113	A.D. 850	750 yrs.	7
Herodotus	480-425 B.C.	A.D. 900	1,300 yrs.	8
Catallus	54 B.C.	A.D. 1550	1,600 yrs.	3
Euripedes	480-406 B.C.	A.D. 1100	1,500 yrs.	9
Aristophanes	450-385 B.C.	A.D. 900	1,200 yrs.	10
Aristotle	384-322 B.C.	A.D. 1100	1,400 yrs.	49
Plato	427-347 B.C.	A.D. 900	1,200 yrs.	7
New Testament	A.D.40-100	A.D. 125	25 yrs.	24,000 +

Now I don't know about you, but I sure find it quite odd that nobody questions the authenticity of Plato's writings when we have only 7 copies, which are 1,200 years from the original! Yet, we have portions of the New Testament within 25 years of the original with tens of thousands of copies, and people still scoff at the Christian who declares that the Bible is accurate and reliable? In fact, we've even recently discovered even more New Testament books that are even closer than that near the same place where they found the Dead Sea Scrolls. Gee, I wonder why they're not telling us about this?

"One of the most exciting finds involves Cave 7. In Cave 7 we have different types of manuscripts. They're written on papyrus rather than parchment or sheepskin, and it is written in Greek not Hebrew or Paleo-Hebrew. Nineteen small fragments of papyrus were found.

Seventeen of the nineteen fragments were unread, and the reason was they had to find them in the Old Testament, and they weren't Old Testament. They were New Testament fragments. One of the most obvious is from Mark, and this particular fragment mentions Genessaret which is a peculiar word for the Sea of Galilee used only in the 1st Century, so this helps date it together with the style of letters.

This is a quotation from Mark 6:52-53 that mentions Genessaret. Well with computers, you can adjust the margins but when you adjust it-BINGO! It fits up and down and sideways with the word Genessaret-that unique first century word right in the middle.

This is Mark 6:52-53. And as they continued to analyze it, they found several other passages from Mark, and Acts, and 1 Timothy and 2 Peter and James verified. And the real significance is necessarily before 68 A.D. before the Romans came in and destroyed all this."[1]

Now put all this together and here's what you get. If you take the 68 AD date there for these New Testament manuscripts, this means we now have portions of the Gospel of Mark within 13 years of the actual time of writing, and it means we have portions of the Book of Romans within 11 years, portions of James within 8 years, Acts within 5 years, 1 Timothy within 5 years, and listen, portions of 2 Peter, the exact same year it was estimated to have been written! And so, I'll say it again. Nobody questions the authenticity of Plato's writings when we have only 7 copies of his that are 1,200 years removed from the original and Aristotle that's 1,400 years removed from the original, and yet, we now have portions of the New Testament within the actual year of its actual writing and people still scoff at the Christian who declares that the Bible is accurate and reliable? This is why one researcher stated this:

"No book from the ancient world comes to us with more abundant evidence for its integrity than does the New Testament. The authenticity and the general integrity of the books of the New Testament may be regarded as finally established."

In other words, it's done! Oh, but that's just the New Testament. How about the Old Testament? How does it hold up? Is it accurate? Is it reliable? Of course, it is. How do we know? Well, this was the amazing discovery of the Dead Sea Scrolls. You see, prior to the discovery of the Dead Sea Scrolls, the earliest copy we had of the Old Testament was from around 900 AD.[2]

But the Dead Sea Scrolls reduced this gap by about 1,000 years to around 125 BC. And since the Dead Sea Scrolls were 1,000 years older than what we previously had, the skeptics couldn't wait to expose all kinds of errors in the Old Testament. So, was there? No! Of course not! In fact, the only variances found were minor things such as punctuation or differences in spelling, and that's because the Qumran community wrote in a different dialect, which changes nothing. Let me show you what I mean. We do it today. Some people spell "Theater" like that but others spell it like this "Theatre." Does that change anything? No! Or some people today spell "Savior" like that but others spell it like this "Saviour." Did that make a major doctrinal difference? No! And so, it is with the Dead Sea Scrolls. These dialectic differences were all minor things like those examples which mean there's no doctrinal variances from what we have today. In fact, they also found an early Book of the Old Testament with the Dead Sea Scrolls, and it too was written within the lifetime of the original. Check this out.

"Well all of these years of copying have to produce changes. Not so. When we understand the way they did it. The way they counted the letters. And then when we compare what was a thousand years earlier from the oldest it's perfect. When we look at the youngest Old Testament book.

Scholars will differ, but conservatively the one that was written latest is about 325 before Christ B.C. The oldest Dead Sea Scroll was written 300 years before Christ. We've got about 25 years separating the original and now Wikipedia suggested that the oldest Dead Sea Scroll was about 325. Well, certainly less than a generation removed from the original we have copies of today. We have dependable text and it's not reasonable to think otherwise."

In other words, it's illogical to doubt that the Bible really came from God. And this is why.

Sir Frederick Kenyon stated this:

"The Christian can take the whole Bible in his hand and say without fear or hesitation that he holds in it the true Word of God, handed down without essential loss from generation throughout the centuries."[3]

This is why you can't have it both ways. You can't accept some books of antiquity that have little or no manuscript data and then turn around and deny the authenticity of the Bible. Why? Because the volumes of manuscript data, the early manuscript data, clearly present the Bible as the genuine Word of God. And anything short of this is called hypocrisy.

The **7th line of logical evidence** showing us that the Bible really did come from God is that **Archaeology Says So.** Let's take a look at just one classic historical passage in the Bible.

Exodus 12:37-38,40-41 "The Israelites journeyed from Rameses to Succoth. There were about six hundred thousand men on foot, besides women and children. Many other people went up with them, as well as large droves of livestock, both flocks and herds. Now the length of time the Israelite people lived in Egypt was 430 years. At the end of the 430 years, to the very day, all the LORD's divisions left Egypt."

And so how do we know that the Bible really did come from God? Well, apparently the 7th line of evidence is that Archaeology says so. What'd we just read? The Israelites went on a literal Exodus, to the literal Promised Land that God was literally giving to them, right? And the reason why this is important is because it records for us an actual historical event that's recorded for us in the Bible. And yet, the skeptics would doubt this and say something like this, "Well, the Bible couldn't have come from God because God can't lie. And since we find historical inaccuracies in the Bible, it couldn't have come from God." And so, the question is, "Is this true? Are there historical inaccuracies in the Bible?" No! In fact, you'll be happy to know that it's been the privileged duty of the archaeologist to silence the mouth of the skeptic. Let's take a look at just a few of the many examples of Old and New Testament!

The Flood:

Many skeptics not only disbelieve the historical account of Noah's Flood, but they even go so far as to say, "Well, if there really was a global flood, then surely there'd be some historical evidence of it outside the Bible." Well guess what? There is! Tons of it! There are about 500 different historical accounts of the flood from around the world. Let's look at just a few of them.

Babylonian accounts, the pre-flood people were giants who became impious and depraved, except one of them who reverenced the gods and was wise and prudent. His name was Noa, and he dwelt with his three sons Sem, Japet, Chem, and their wives Tidea, Pandora, Noela, and Noegla. Noa foresaw the destruction and began building an ark. 78 years later, the oceans, inland seas, and rivers burst forth from below, along with many days of violent rain. The waters overflowed all the mountains, and the human race was drowned except Noa and his family who survived on his ship. The ship came to rest at last on the top of a mountain.

Ancient Chinese writings refers to a violent catastrophe that occurred to the earth. One Chinese classic, called *Hihking*, tells the story of Fuhi, whom the Chinese consider to be the father of their civilization. This history records that Fuhi, his wife, three sons and three daughters escaped the great flood. He and his family were the only people left alive on earth, and they repopulated the world. In fact, in an ancient temple in China there is a wall painting that shows Fuhi's boat and the picture shows the boat in raging waters with dolphins swimming around it and a dove with an olive branch in his beak is flying back towards the boat.

A Hawaiian account says that long after the death of the first man, the world became a wicked and terrible place to live. There was one good man left, his name was Nu-u. He made a great canoe with a house on it and filled it with animals. The water came up all over the earth and killed all the people. Only Nu-u and his family were saved.

Discovered in the histories of the **Toltec Indians** of ancient Mexico, is a story of the first world that they say lasted 1,716 years and was destroyed by a great flood that covered even the highest mountains. Their story tells of a man named Tapi who was a very pious man. The creator told Tapi to build a boat that he would live in and escape the destruction. He was told that he should take his wife, a pair of every animal that was alive into this boat. Naturally everyone thought he was crazy. Then the rain started, and the flood came. The men and animals tried to climb the mountains, but the mountains became flooded as well. Finally, the rain ended, and Tapi decided that the water had dried up, so he let loose a dove. Following the great flood, people began to multiply and built a very high great tower, to provide a safe place in case the world were destroyed again. However, everyone started to speak different languages, and the people became confused and wandered to other parts of the world.[4]

In fact, other cultures also speak of this confusion of the languages. **Sumerian** tablets record for us, *"There was a golden age when all mankind spoke the same language. Speech was then confused by the god, the lord of wisdom."*

And the **Babylonians** also had a similar account which states, *"The gods destroyed a temple tower and scattered them abroad and made their speech strange."*

The Black Stele: Skeptics claimed that Moses could not have been the author of the Pentateuch for writing was supposedly not developed during his time. However, thanks to the discovery of the Black Stele, which contained the "written" form of the laws of Hammurabi, writing was in fact commonplace during Moses' time just like the Bible states. And speaking of writing, according to the Harvard Chinese-Japanese Library, written Chinese dates back to approximately 2500 B.C., which just so happens to be pretty close to the time of the end of the flood. And this is when all languages would have had their origin. Now what's amazing is that the Chinese language is not only a pictorial language, but it hasn't changed much over the passage of time and oddly enough, these Chinese "picture words" speak about Noah's flood. See for yourself.

• The Chinese word for *boat* is depicted by eight mouths (eight people) inside a container.

• The Chinese word for *total* is a uniting of eight people, who join hands over the earth.

• The word for *empty* is made up of two words, *cave* and *work. Cave* is depicted as eight people under one roof. Some would say this shows that when Noah and his family left the ark, they first moved into a *cave* for shelter, hence eight people under one roof.

• Then, they left the *cave* each day to *work* at *emptying* the ark and then share this post-flood experience with future generations, which eventually found its way into the Chinese language.

• The Chinese character for *devil* is formed from three other characters: man, garden, and private. **(Genesis 3:1-7)**

• The words *rebellion* and *confusion* link together the words for tongue and walking. **(Genesis 11:4-9)**

• And finally, the word for *garden* or *field* is a square and inside the square are four straight lines radiating outward in a "plus sign" shape. According to **Genesis**

2, a river in the Garden of Eden flowed outward in four streams and watered the entire garden.

The Patriarchs: Skeptics want to say that the Biblical account of the Patriarchs is totally unfounded. But thanks to the discovery of the Ebla archives in northern Syria in the 1970's, we now know that the Biblical account of the Patriarchs is not only accurate and true, but even the personal names and places mentioned by the Patriarchs is accurate as well.

Doors in Sodom: Skeptics claimed that doors as were mentioned in the account of Lot in Sodom were not in use during that time in that culture. However, thanks to the discoveries of archaeologists, we now know that doors were used then as a means of protection just like the Bible states. In fact, many skeptics would also deny the destruction of Sodom and Gomorrah and say that there is no evidence of this event.

But that's not true, because we not only have discovered the ruins of Sodom and Gomorrah near the Dead Sea, but both places were obviously destroyed by an enormous fire and debris is about 3 feet thick with brimstone and ash found throughout the area.

Camels: Skeptics claimed that the account of camels in the Book of Genesis is false for they were not utilized back in those times However, thanks to the discoveries of archaeologists, we now know that the usage of camels was indeed commonplace just like the Bible states.

The Hittites: Skeptics claimed that there were no such people as the Hittites, which are mentioned in the Old Testament. However, thanks to the discoveries of archaeologists, we now know that the Hittites were a real people and even now have records of over 1,200 years of their civilization, just like the Bible states.

Solomon's Wealth: Many skeptics think that the Biblical references to King Solomon's wealth are greatly exaggerated. But we now know that wealth in antiquity was in fact concentrated with the king and so Solomon's prosperity was entirely feasible.

King Sargon: It was once claimed by skeptics that there was no such Assyrian King called Sargon that the Bible talks about in Isaiah. But we have not only discovered Sargon's palace in Iraq, but even the very event that Isaiah recorded for us in Chapter 20 about Sargon's capture of Ashdod, is recorded there on his palace as well.

Various Battles: Skeptics also want to discount the various historical battles that are mentioned in the Bible. But thanks to archaeology, we now know that once again the Bible is right.

• The military campaign into Israel by Pharaoh is recorded on the temple walls in Thebes, Egypt.

• The revolt of Moab against Israel is recorded on the Mesha inscription.

• The fall of Samaria to Sargon II is also recorded on his palace walls.

• The campaign of the Assyrian King Sennacherib against Judah is recorded on the Taylor Prism.

• The siege of Lachish also by Sennacherib is recorded on the Lachish reliefs.

• The assassination of Sennacherib by his own sons is recorded in the annals of his son Esarhaddon.

• The fall of Nineveh is recorded on the tablet of Nabopolasar.

• The fall of Jerusalem to Nebuchadnezzar King of Babylon is recorded in the Babylonian Chronicles.

• The captivity of Jehoiachin King of Judah is recorded on the Babylonian Ration Records.

• The fall of Babylon to the Medes and Persians is recorded on the Cyrus Cylinder.

• And the freeing of the captives in Babylon by Cyrus the Great is also recorded on the Cyrus Cylinder.

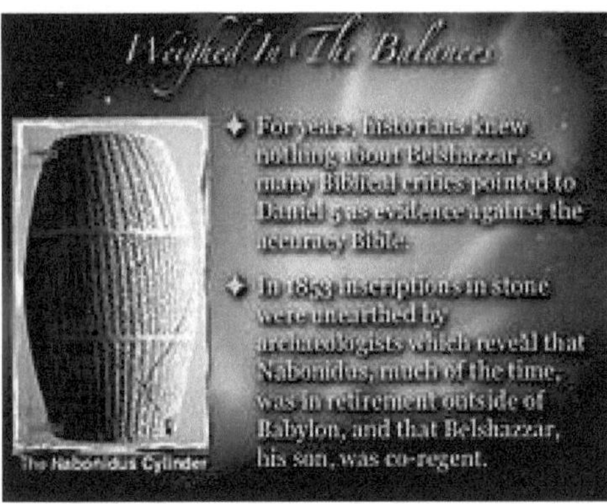

Belshazzar: Skeptics claimed that there was no such person as Belshazzar as is mentioned in the Book of Daniel. However, thanks to the discoveries of archaeologists, we now know that he existed and ruled in Babylon just like the Bible states. And we even found tablets that showed how Belshazzar was in fact Nabonidus' son who served as co-regent in Babylon. Therefore, when he offered Daniel the "third highest ruler position in the kingdom" for reading the handwriting on the wall, it would've been legitimate. It was the next highest available position.

Various Figures: Many skeptics not only doubt Belshazzar, but they even doubt many people mentioned throughout the Bible. Yet, over 50 persons named in the Old Testament and 27 persons in the New Testament, including some of their likenesses are known from other records outside the Bible.

The Exodus: Many skeptics want to say that there is absolutely no evidence whatsoever of the 2 million Israelites making a trek through the desert like the Bible states. Yet if that's true why do they find chariot wheels at the bottom of the Red Sea? Let's take a look:

"The formations at Nuweiba Beach are generally smaller and scattered randomly across the sea floor. Divers familiar with the area have compared the distribution of coral here to a junkyard and the aftermath of a disaster. Since the earliest explorations at Nuweiba, one distinctive type of formation has often been identified on the sea floor.

A slender table like structure, sometimes standing on end with a coral encrusted base. A straight shaft and a circular top. It's a 90-degree angle. A right angle between something that looks like an axle and the wheel.

You can see this in different varieties and looks very different from normal coral growth and it is like a manmade structure with coral growth on it.

While most of the possible artifacts found off the coast of Nuweiba are covered with coral. One significant discovery was not. There's one find that the Nuweiba location that is of great interest, and that is the gilded wheel. It is a wooden basic structure of the wheel and it's covered with gold or electrum-which is a mixture of silver and gold; and corals have not been able to grow on it. It's been very well preserved, although it's very fragile.

It seems like the wooden content has been dissolved so you could break it if you would try to remove it. After it's discovery, the fragile, wheel-shaped veneer was photographed then left in place on the sea floor. Later analysis revealed that it's dimensions and design resembled four spoke chariot wheels painted on an 18th Dynasty tomb wall near the biblical date of the Exodus."

But that's not all. They not only find human and horse remains down there, but they also find clear evidence of the Israelites journey, after the Red Sea crossing, well into the desert. Check this out:

Search for the Real Mt. Sinai/Horeb:

Narrator: *"Now across, the explorers felt comfortable that they have found strong evidence of the crossing of the Exodus, but with a foreboding desert stretched before them, the question remained -Where did the children of Israel go from here."*

Bob Cornuke: *"At first, they got out on the other side and they rejoiced. The Bible says they went 3 days into the wilderness and they found the bitter springs of Marah 'for three days they traveled in the desert when they came to Marah, they could not drink its water because it was bitter.'* **Exodus 15:22-23a** *They should have stopped at the springs along the way, some bitter water springs."*

"Sure enough, we found these springs, sitting right there by the road and we went over and tasted the water and it was so bitter you couldn't touch it to your tongue. We opened the Bible and we started thumbing through the pages-we're thinking, 'What are we going to see next?' and the Bible tells us they came to the 70 palms and 12 springs of Elim." ('...they came to Elim, where there were twelve springs and 70 palm trees...' **Exodus 15:27**)

John Williams: **"***As we were driving along there's a whole bunch of palms, a whole bunch of springs-and this like really, really blew me away."*

Cornuke: "*And within the palm trees we found several springs of clear water, bubbling up out of the ground. Now today they have put these concrete encasements around the springs so that the water doesn't seep out into the sand, but we did find evidence of 12 springs of water bubbling up out of the ground as the Bible says amongst the palm trees."*

Narrator: "*What would come next would be a surprise. God's command to Moses was to strike the rock at Horeb, and water would come gushing for his thirsty nation. Could this have really happened? Would there be any evidence remaining of this? And most important, could this rock still be in existence?"*

Cornuke: *"It must have been a very pronounced rock, because the Bible describes it as the split rock at Horeb. You would have been able to see it from* *miles away. A very unique rock, and there was a very unique rock indeed there. Right on the west side of the mountain.*

It goes up 40 feet from this knoll area, and it has this fracture right down the middle. It goes from top to bottom about 9 inches wide. Below this rock, you can see where this rock has washed smooth. That it came out in millions, and maybe billions of gallons of water that poured forth over these rocks.

This is not sandstone. This is dense granite rock the water has rushed over, thus making it smooth now. This part of the world only gets a 1/2 inch of rain every 10 years. It's impossible for this little rainfall to wash away an entire mountainside and make the granite boulders smooth."

Narrator: *"Evidence was mounting. But how would the Israelites get enough water for an entire nation of perhaps 2 million people?"*

Cornuke: *"They would have needed a lake of water because they had up to 2 million people possibly. We found an area that water came in and filled up this granite basin and it filled it up and it was several acres in size."*

Narrator: *"Like a puzzle, the pieces were all fitting together. But what would they discover at the top of Jabel el Lawz. If this was the holy mountain that God touched. What would they find?"*

Cornuke: *"We saw looming up in front of us, this mountain, about 8,000-foot peak -Jabel el Lawz -and the very unique thing about the top of it, is that it's black on the top."*

Williams: *"Why is the top of this mountain black and none of the other mountains around there black on the top? And it's like such an unusual visual image."*

Cornuke: *"And we were drawn to climb this mountain to see what these unique black rocks were."*

Williams: "*And so the climb began, and we eventually got there."*

Cornuke: *"When we got to the top, we found these rocks that were blackened on the outside. They were shiny black as if some kind of external heat source melted them."*

Williams: *"Which fits again scripture that says that this mountain was touched by God and by fire and lightening, and whatever, so it would make sense it would be blackened."*

Cornuke: *"And God said He descended on the mountain and flames of furnace." ("Mount Sinai was covered with smoke, because the LORD descended on it in fire. The smoke billowed up from it like smoke from flames a furnace."* ~**Exodus 19:18A)**

Cornuke: "*So, Larry said, 'Hey they may be volcanic.' So, I took a big rock and I slammed it down on top of another one and we broke off a chunk of this. We were amazed when we looked at this rock. It was melted, crusty on the outside- but it was granite on the inside and we broke other rocks in the area, and sure enough all them, they were melted black on top and were granite on the inside."*

Luke's Census: Skeptics claimed that the account in Luke's gospel of the census is nowhere to be found in Roman records. However, thanks to the discoveries of archaeologists, we now know that this kind of census taking was commonplace during that time just like the Bible states.

Pontius Pilate: Skeptics claimed that there are no Roman records of Pontius Pilate ruling in Judea. However, thanks to the discoveries of archaeologists, we now know that Pontius Pilate was not only a real person but also ruling in Judea just like the Bible states. In 1961 Italian archaeologists were excavating an ancient Roman amphitheatre near Caesarea and uncovered an interesting limestone block. On the face of it is an inscription of a dedication to Tiberius Caesar that says that it was from "Pontius Pilate, Prefect of Judea."

The Pool of Bethesda: Skeptics claimed that there is no evidence for this pool that's mentioned in the Bible where Jesus healed the crippled man. However, thanks to the discoveries of archaeologists, we now know that the pool of Bethesda was not only real but also right where it is supposed to be just like the Bible states.

Seat of Moses: Skeptics claimed that the mentioning of this type of seat mentioned in the Bible must be figurative because there is no evidence of its actual existence. However, thanks to the discoveries of archaeologists, we now know that the seat of Moses was an actual seat that was made of stone where the teacher of a synagogue would have sat just like the Bible states.

Caiaphas: He was not only the high priest for 18 years, but it was this same Caiaphas that Jesus was taken to after He was arrested, and he asked Jesus, "Are you the Christ or Messiah, the Son of the Blessed One?" to which Jesus replied, "I AM." Then he handed Jesus over to Pilate to be tried. Well, he's not only real, but his family tomb was recently discovered by accident by construction workers who were making a road just south of the Old City of Jerusalem.

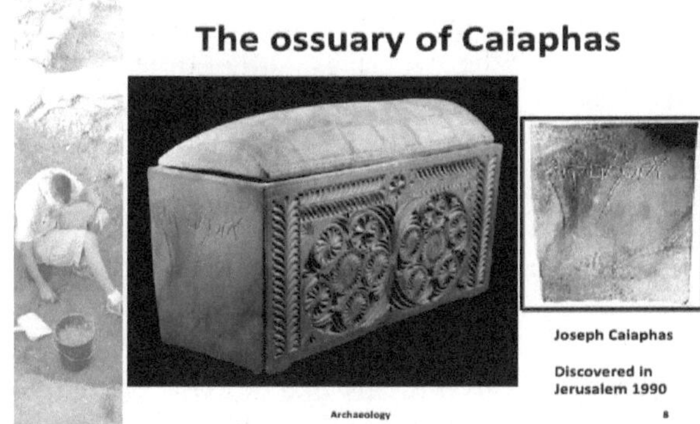

Archaeologists were called to the scene and they found ossuaries (limestone bone boxes) with the remains of Caiaphas' family including himself. The most beautifully decorated one was inscribed with his name and sure enough inside were the remains of a 60-year-old man, almost certainly to be those of the same Caiaphas mentioned in the N.T. As one-man states, "This remarkable discovery has, for the first time, provided us with the actual physical remains of an actual character mentioned in the Bible."

And here's the point. Now contrast this with the Book of Mormon who would have you and I believe that their so-called "New" New Testament of Jesus Christ is also reliable and accurate like the Bible. Really? I don't think so. And the reason why is because it doesn't hold up at all to archaeology. Let's take a look at what so-called archaeological evidence there is for the Book of Mormon, and you tell me if we should trust the thing. Let's take a look.

Metallurgy: The Book of Mormon describes the various usages of iron, steel, brass, and various metals in the Americas before the birth of Jesus Christ. The problem is that archaeology has shown that metallurgy did not appear in the Americas until about the 9th century A.D.

Weapons of War: The Book of Mormon describes the presence of chariots and other various weaponry that was supposed to have been used in the New World according to their dates. The problem is, archeologists have found neither the evidence of chariots nor other weapons mentioned in the Book of Mormon at this time.

Major Battles: The Hill Cumorah in New York is described by the Book of Mormon to be the location of two major wars that involved the deaths of millions of people. However, no remains or even weapons of these wars have ever been found there.

Crops & Agriculture: The Book of Mormon describes the various agriculture of the Americas as being similar to that found in Biblical times in the Middle East. But the problem is archaeology has shown that the Americas, at that time, didn't grow that kind of crops and what crops they did grow are not mentioned in the Book of Mormon.

Use of Linen and Silk: The Book of Mormon describes the use of linen and silk in the New World at their time, but neither silk nor linen items have ever been found during this time frame.

Animals: The Book of Mormon describes various animals like donkey, cattle, oxen, and even elephants; as living in the Americas at their time frame. But the problem is, none of these animals ever existed in North America, Central America, or even South America during the time the Book of Mormon mentions.

DNA: The Book of Mormon actually says that the Native American population is descendants of their ancestors called the Lamanites, who originated from ancient Israel around 2,600 years ago. The problem is DNA samples have proven beyond the shadow of a doubt that the Native American peoples are descendants from Siberian and Asian ancestors, not made up Mormon tribes. Furthermore, there is also no archaeological evidence for the other mythical Mormon tribe called the "Nephites," who were supposed to be the "white & exceedingly fair people."

I don't know about you, but it appears to me that somebody's making up a story, unlike the Bible, how about you? And this is why this person has this to say about the importance of Biblical Archaeology.

Dr. Norman Geisler: *"We find that there is good evidence that from archaeology that the Scriptures speak the truth. In many instances, the Scriptures even reflect firsthand knowledge of the times and customs it describes. While many have doubted the accuracy of the Bible, time and continued research have consistently demonstrated that the Word of God is better informed than its critics. In fact, while thousands of finds from the ancient world support in broad outline and often in detail the biblical picture, not one incontrovertible find has ever contradicted the Bible."*

Why? Because it came from God and He doesn't lie, even when it comes to history! And this is why you can't have it both ways. You cannot agree with some of the Bible's teaching and then turn around and deny its authenticity. Why? Because the historical integrity of the Bible as verified by archaeology proves it's the genuine Word of God. And anything short of this is called hypocrisy. And so, it is with the skeptics of the Bible! They spout off bold claims that the Bible cannot be trusted, it's a book full of errors, it's whooped up by man, yet it is they who refuse to look at the evidence. People be encouraged today! You don't have to give into the attacks of the skeptic. You don't have to give into doubt. You don't have to give into one iota of criticism! What we hold in our hands is the genuine Word of God! And that's why, more than ever, we've got to wake up and realize the golden opportunity that God is giving us. Our world is in a frantic search for purpose and direction and meaning to life. They realize the world is messed up and it's getting worse! And so, they're full of questions like, "Why do I exist? Where did I come from? Where is all this evil coming from? Is there life after death? And is there any hope?" And its high time that we the Church get busy not just *saying* the Bible came from God, but *showing* the world that it came from God, and the way we do that is by putting our lives on the line for it, like these Christians did. Risking death for God's Word:

"6.2 Million Seekers long for a bible in their own language. Their lands are closed to evangelism, but their hearts are open to God's truth. There are no Christian bookstores. No place to get a bible. To ask is to risk your life. And yet, 17,000 dare to ask every day. Considering the Word of God more precious than their own lives. How about you?"

Yes, how about us? Once again, if we expect our world to believe us when we tell them about Jesus, and God's Trustworthy Words that are contained within the Bible, that has all the answers they're looking for, then we too need to put our lives on the line for it, NOT keep leaving it on the kitchen table collecting dust.

Chapter Five

Bible Prophecy Says So

"Once there was a really terrible flood. Everybody made it to safety except one guy. He climbs on top of his house and the water is lapping at his feet when a helicopter flies overhead and drops down a rope and the pilot says, "Climb up."

But the man yells back to the pilot, "Hey, it's all right. The Lord is going to save me." And the helicopter flew away.

But then the water began to rise higher and higher and then a boat came by and again the man said, "NO, NO, go away. The Lord will come and save me." So, the boat sped off.

The water was getting seriously deep by now and fortunately another helicopter comes by and drops down the rope. Again, he says, "I don't need saving. My Lord will come and save me. Reluctantly the second helicopter flies off.

The rain continues to pour down and the water continues to rise and unfortunately the man drowns. So, he's at the gate of Heaven and he sees St. Peter and the man is so confused. So, he asks St. Peter, "What's up with this? What's going on? I've lived the life of a faithful Born-Again Christian. Why didn't you rescue me?

St. Peter replied, "We sent you two helicopters and a boat."

So, as you can see obviously this man needed help. How many can say he learned the hard way. God will send you his provision for your needs, you just need to reach out and take it the first time. Believe it or not, it's not just this man being flooded on top of his house, but it is the same thing with the Bible. Everything we need is right in this book, the Bible. But unfortunately, all we need to do is just reach out and take it the first time. We get drowned, as Christians, by our circumstances. Therefore, there is one mistake that you and I as Christians should never make, concerning the Bible, never ever doubt that the Bible came from God. But this has been going on with Christians and non-Christians alike. It doesn't seem to matter today, due to an ongoing skepticism for more than a century and false criticism towards the Bible, people even Christians, are starting to doubt that the Bible really came from God. In order to stave off this criticism and hypocrisy even in the church, unfortunately, we are going to continue with *Did the Bible Really Come from God?* So far, we have seen the 7 lines of logical evidence which are:

The Bible says so
Jesus says so
Apostles say so
History says so
Transmission standards say so
Manuscript says so
Archaeology says so

So not only do we have copies of the Bible within the actual year of its writing, unlike secular writings that no body questions, like Plato and Aristotle, 1,200 and 1,400 years removed, but we have archaeology that proves it came from God, He is Holy, and He cannot lie. They say it has historic inaccuracies, but that's not true. Archaeology proves that everything that God says is right on even historical accounts, even with the people of Israel going through the Red Sea. We saw the chariots that were destroyed, under the sea.

The **8th line of logical evidence** showing us that the Bible really did come from God is that **Bible Prophecy Says So.** If the book came from God, you would think that it would contain things that only God would know. Which would be the future. But don't take my word for it. Let's listen to God's.

Isaiah 42:5-9 "This is what God the LORD says – He who created the heavens and stretched them out, who spread out the earth and all that comes out of it, who gives breath to its people, and life to those who walk on it: I, the LORD, have called you in righteousness; I will take hold of your hand. I will keep you and will make you to be a covenant for the people and a light for the Gentiles, to open eyes that are blind, to free captives from prison and to release from the dungeon those who sit in darkness. I am the LORD; that is my name! I will not give my glory to another or my praise to idols. See, the former things have taken place, and new things I declare; before they spring into being I announce them to you."

So how do we know that the Bible really did come from God? Well, apparently, the 8th line of evidence is that *Prophecy* says so. What'd we just read? God is not only the Creator of all things, but He knows about all things before they ever even happen, right? And the way He demonstrates that is by recording for us these prophetic events, i.e. the future, before it even happens, right? Which, as we saw before, is radically different than the so-called psychics out there that have a horrible track record of getting 92% of things wrong, God on the other hand, when He makes a prediction about the future, is not only 100% accurate, but 100% accurate all the time! AND, it deals with specific intimate details right down to the tee! Not like the psychics that say, "You're going to meet somebody new," and you live in downtown New York City, DUH! And, whether you realize it or not, this aspect of God, prophesying future events 100% accurate before they ever even occur is yet another powerful way to demonstrate that the Bible really did come from God. Why? Because stop and think about it. If a book were to have really come from God then one would expect that it would contain things that only God could know, right? And so, the question is, "Does the Bible contain things that only God would know?" Absolutely! In fact, it doesn't contain just a few things but tons of things only God could know. Let me share just a few of them with you.

The **1st thing that God accurately prophesies 100%** of the time showing us that the Bible really did come from Him is **The Rise and Fall of Nations.**

Daniel 2:36,38,39-40,45 "That was the dream, and now I'll tell you what it means...You are the head of gold. After you are gone, another kingdom will rule, but it won't be as strong. Then it will be followed by a kingdom of bronze that will rule the whole world. Next, a kingdom of iron will come to power, crushing and shattering everything...God has told you what is going to happen."

And boy did God ever tell Nebuchadnezzar what was going to happen. What we see here is Daniel's amazing prophecy of the rise of 4 totally different nations existing hundreds of years apart from each other. The 1st kingdom was Nebuchadnezzar's or Babylon, the 2nd was the Medo-Persian empire, the 3rd was the Grecian empire with Alexander the Great, and the 4th was the Roman empire which will be revived in the last days. And you may not think this is a big deal, but the skeptics sure do. You see, even the skeptics readily admit that Daniel accurately predicted the rise of these 4 empires, right down to the tee. In fact, so much so, that they try to deny it's supernatural origin by claiming that the Book of Daniel was written after the events took place. But of course, this doesn't hold up to the textual evidence and it only reveals what the skeptics are really saying, "Don't confuse me with the facts. That's not possible. Only God could do that." Uh huh! And He did! [1]

But that's not all. The Bible not only accurately predicted the rise of nations, but it also predicted their downfall. And by the way, many of them were destroyed because of their ill-treatment of the Jewish people. I think there's a lesson there. For instance, the Bible specifically predicted in the Book of Nahum that the nation of Nineveh would be permanently destroyed, be destroyed by fire, would easily be captured, their army officers would desert, and that they'd even be drunk in their final hours. And so, the question is, "Did God get it right? Of course, God doesn't lie! He's 100% accurate all the time!

Not only did Nineveh cease to exist shortly after this prophecy, but just like Nahum said, archaeologists have uncovered a layer of ash in its ruins showing it was destroyed by fire, and ancient Babylonian records reveal that Nineveh was easily overtaken and that their officers fled the scene, and a Greek historian even records for us that "The king gave much wine to his soldiers that night" which caused them to be drunk.[2]

But Nineveh isn't the only nation the Bible predicted would fall. The Book of Isaiah predicted that the nation of Babylon would specifically be overthrown and attacked by the Medes, their gates would open for a guy named Cyrus, and they would be reduced to swampland. And so again, the question is, "Did God get it right? Of course, God doesn't lie! He's 100% accurate all the time! Today it's common knowledge that the Medes joined up with the Persians and conquered Babylon, and despite Babylon's incredible defenses, history records that a guy named Cyrus diverted the flow of the Euphrates River and marched into the city via the riverbed, and archaeological excavations reveal that parts of Babylon cannot be dug up because its now under the water, making it swamp-like.

In the Books of Ezekiel and Amos predicted that the city of Tyre would specifically be attacked by many nations, it's fortresses would fail, their stones, timber and soil would be thrown into the sea, and the remains of the city would be used "to spread fishing nets." Now that's a lot of specifics! So, did God get it right? Of course, He doesn't lie! Babylon was the first to overthrow the city of Tyre, but the people retreated to an island fortress away from the mainland and escaped total destruction. So, wait a second, did God get it wrong? No! He wasn't done yet. Almost 250 years later, Alexander the Great attacked the city of Tyre. And when he did, the people did the same thing. They ran out to their island fortress.

But as history records, Alexander the Great took the rubble from Tyre's mainland ruins, "the stones, timber and soil" and cast them into the sea to make a land bridge to the island and conquered the people. In fact, the city of Tyre was repeatedly destroyed by the Phoenicians, the Romans, the Crusaders, and even the Muslims.

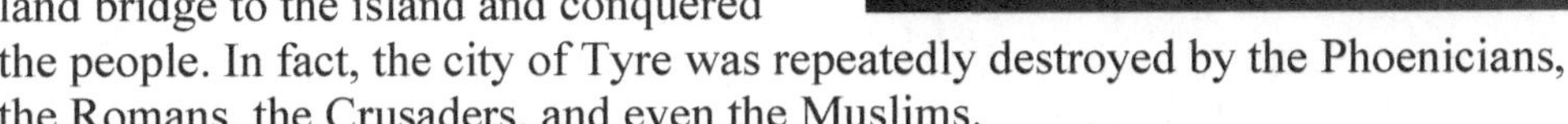

And today Tyre is nothing but a flat barren rock that people only use "to spread their fishing nets." Now I'm not a rocket scientist, but I'd say there's no way somebody could know all that specific information about the rise and fall of all those nations in advance without some outside help, how about you? That can't happen by chance. In fact, the only way they could know is if somebody who was above and beyond time and knew the beginning from the end personally told them about it, right? Hmmm. I wonder who that might be? God perhaps? And that's one of the reasons why we know the Bible came from Him![3]

The **2nd thing God prophesies** 100% accurate all the time showing us the Bible really did come from Him is **The Arrival of the Messiah.**

Isaiah 7:13-14 "Then Isaiah said, "Hear now, you house of David! Is it not enough to try the patience of men? Will you try the patience of my God also? Therefore, the Lord himself will give you a sign: The virgin will be with child and will give birth to a son and will call him Immanuel."

Now, we're all very familiar with Isaiah's prophecy that the Messiah would be born of a virgin. I mean, we hear about it almost every single Christmas. In fact, we hear about it so much, that I think we have lost its significance. But here's the point. As amazing as the virgin birth is, that's only one of hundreds of prophecies that Jesus fulfilled, proving that He was indeed, the Messiah. Let's take a look at just 30 of them.

1. Born of a virgin (Isaiah 7:14)
2. Born of the seed of Abraham, Isaac, Jacob (Genesis 12,17; Numbers 24)
3. Descended from the tribe of Judah (Genesis 49)
4. Heir to the throne of David (Isaiah 9:7)
5. Born in Bethlehem (Micah 5:2)
6. Slaughter of the innocents (Jeremiah 31:15)
7. Flight to Egypt (Hosea 11:1)
8. Proceeded by a forerunner (Isaiah 40:3-5; Malachi 3:1)
9. Declared the Son of God (Psalm 2:7)
10. Galilean ministry (Isaiah 9:1-2)
11. Came to heal the brokenhearted (Isaiah 61:1-2)
12. Rejected by His own (Isaiah 53:3)
13. Triumphal entry (Zechariah 9:9)
14. Betrayed by a friend (Psalm 41:9)
15. Sold for 30 pieces of silver (Zechariah 11:12-13)
16. Accused by false witnesses (Psalm 35:11)
17. Silent to accusations (Isaiah 53:7)
18. Spat upon and smitten (Isaiah 50:6)
19. Hated without reason (Psalm 35:19)
20. Hands pierced (Psalm 22:16)
21. Crucified with transgressors (Isaiah 53:12)

22. Scorned and mocked (Psalm 22:7-8)
23. Given vinegar and gall (Psalm 69:21)
24. Prayer for His enemies (Psalm 109:4)
25. Soldiers gambled for His coat (Psalm 22:18)
26. No bones broken (Psalm 34:20)
27. Side pierced (Zechariah 12:10)
28. Buried with the rich (Isaiah 53:9)
29. Would rise from the dead (Psalm 16:10; 49:15)
30. Would ascend to God's right hand (Psalm 68:18)

Now here's the point. For one person to specifically fulfill all those prophecies is not only amazing, that God is screaming out, "It really came from me!" But I still don't think we catch just how amazing it is until we take a look at the odds of something like this taking place.

"By using the modern science of probability, we find that the chance that any man might have lived down to the present time and fulfilled just eight prophecies is 1 in 10 to the 17th power. In order to help us comprehend this staggering probability, it can be illustrated by taking silver dollars and laying them on the state of Texas, which would be enough to cover the state 2 feet deep.

Now mark one of these silver dollars with a "red X" and stir the whole mass thoroughly, all over the state. Blindfold a man and tell him that he can travel as far as he wishes, but he must pick up one silver dollar and say that this is the right one. What chance would he have of getting the right one? Just the same chance that the prophets would have had of writing just 8 prophecies and having them all come true in any one man.

Furthermore, the odds of just 48 prophecies being fulfilled in one man would be 1 in 10157. And to give you an idea of just how big of a number that is, the estimated number of electrons in the whole universe is around 1 in 1079."[4]

Now I'm not a rocket scientist, but I'd say it's pretty obvious that there's no way that Jesus fulfilled 48 prophecies by accident. And by the way, He didn't fulfill just 48 but *over 300*. That can't happen by chance. In fact, the only way it could happen is if somebody was above and beyond time and knew the beginning from the end and orchestrated the whole thing. Hmmm. I wonder who that might be? God perhaps? And that's why we know the Bible came from Him! But that's still not all. The Bible also predicted in the Book of Daniel *centuries before it happened,* the long-awaited arrival of the Messiah in Jerusalem. And not just a good guess either, but down to *the exact day*! Daniel predicted in Daniel 9 that 173,880 days from the decree to rebuild Jerusalem, that the Messiah would come to Jerusalem and be cut off from His people. Now that's pretty specific, don't you think? So, what happened 173,880 days after the decree to rebuild Jerusalem? Well, that puts us as March 30 AD 33. And can anyone guess what happened on that day? Hey, that's right! That's the *exact day* when Jesus made His triumphal entry into Jerusalem, and He was rejected, or cut off, from His people! But that still not all. The Bible also predicted many specific events that would occur just prior to the return of the Messiah, His Second Coming, and you tell me if we're not getting close to those. Let's take a look at just 30 of them.

1. Israel Return to the Land Again (Isaiah 43:5-6)
2. Israel Become a Nation Again (Isaiah 11:11-12)
3. Israel Become a Nation Again in One Day (Isaiah 66:8)
4. Israel Become a United Nation (Ezekiel 37:21-22)
5. Israel Have a Powerful Military (Zechariah 12:6)
6. Their Currency Would Become the Shekel (Ezekiel 45:12,13,16)
7. Israel Blossom as a Rose in the Desert (Isaiah 35:1-2)
8. Israel Become a Source of World Conflict (Zechariah 12:2-3)
9. Israel Rebuild the Temple (Revelation 11:2)
10. Increase of Travel (Daniel 12:4)
11. Increase of Knowledge (Daniel 12:4)
12. Increase of Unrest (2 Timothy 3:1,7)
13. Increase of Earthquakes (Matthew 24:7)
14. Increase of Famines (Matthew 24:7)
15. Increase of Pestilence (Luke 21:11)
16. Increase of Wars (Matthew 24:6-7)
17. Increase of Strange Events in the Sky (Luke 21:10-11)
18. Increase of Global Catastrophes (Joel 2:30-31)
19. Increase of False Christs (Matthew 24:4-5)
20. Increase of False Teachers (Matthew 24:11)
21. Increase of Wickedness (2 Timothy 3:1-5)
22. The Church Would go into Apostasy (1 Timothy 4:1-2)
23. The World would Push for a One World Religion (Revelation 13)
24. The People of God Would be Persecuted Around the Whole Planet (Matthew 24:9)
25. There'd be a Rise of an Antichrist & False Prophet (Revelation 13)
26. There'd be a Push for a One World Government (Revelation 13)

27. There's Arise a Global Big Brother Society (Revelation 13)
28. There'd be a Push for a One World Economy (Revelation 13)
29. One Man Would Control all the Buying and Selling on the Planet (Revelation 13)
30. There'd be a Push for Some Sort of a Mark of the Beast to be put in people's Right Hand or Forehead across the Planet (Revelation 13)

I don't know about you, but it's a good thing we don't see any signs of those things taking place! Yeah right! Every single one of them is happening *right now*, which means Jesus is about to come back! In fact, there's almost 2,000 prophecies mentioned in the Bible. 1/3rd of the Bible's content deals with predictive prophecy, all of which has already been fulfilled, as you just saw, or is on the verge of being so. Therefore, here's the point. It doesn't take a rocket scientist to figure out that if all the 300 prophecies came to pass concerning Jesus' 1st Coming, and He knocked them out of the park, then what do you think is going to happen to some 318 prophecies concerning His 2nd Coming? I think He's going to knock those out of the park too! And speaking of Jesus' 2nd Coming, as you clearly saw, the Bible predicted nearly 2,000 years ago that there would be some sort of Mark of the Beast or Antichrist that would be implanted in people all across the planet, right? And this Mark would allow them to buy or sell, right? Well here's the point. I'm glad that's nowhere near on the horizon…or is it? You tell me if we're not getting close for the Return of Jesus Christ, because the commercials for the Mark of the Beast type technology are already here! They're being aired on TV. Check it out for yourself.

"To think something so small (showing a hand holding an RFID chip between their fingers) can connect you to everything that matters, when your life and all you love are on the line. Healthlink is always with you. When every second counts in the emergency room. (shows a scanner scanning an RFID chip. Then info's profile of Robert Jones pops up on a computer screen) Providing immediate access to your medical records.

Because Bob has trouble remembering all his medications.
Because I'm in love with my kid's kids.
Because my car lost control while driving.
Because now I'm looking out for both of us.
Because I have diabetes, but it doesn't have me.
Because I spend my life in the E.R. trying to save yours
HEALTHLINK. LINKING YOU AND YOUR HEALTH RECORD.[4]

Huh? If only you'd receive this implant, it'll save your life. Aren't you glad they're taking over the Health Care System? Notice where they're starting? But they'll never force us into taking that, will they? We'll get to that in a second, but here's my point. Looks to me like somebody's promoting some sort of a mark thingy to implant into our bodies, how about you? Right now, on TV! I mean, won't it be so wonderful, so safe, so convenient? And that's precisely the selling point. And by the way, this same technology has the ability to not only store your medical information, but any information, including your ID, as well as make financial transactions, you know, buy and sell stuff. But you might be thinking, "Hey man, there's no way in the world people are going to accept that thing into their bodies! I don't care what they do! I don't care how many commercials they run, nobody's going to fall for this! This is crazy!" Really? Well crazy or not, you tell me if people, for the first time on mankind's history, are ready to receive some sort of a Mark into their bodies.

Bobby Harley - CBS News: "A procedure that only takes seconds to carry out."

Doctor: "And the chip is now extruded, and we're finished."

Bobbi Harley: "Has turned the Jacobs family into medical pioneers. They are the first people to get chipped. Implanted with a tiny device called a VeriChip that emits radio frequencies. It's a personal I.D. that also contains vital medical information."

Derek Jacobs: "It can save a lot of lives including my Dad's, because he has a lot of medical problems and I want him to be around for a while."

Bobbie Harley: "A hand held scanner reads the VeriChip. Theoretically police, paramedics, and hospital workers would use the information during an emergency. Thousands of Americans are already lining up to get them, and Applied Digital Solutions, the company that developed the VeriChip says this might only be the beginning. Company scientists are already working on a Global Positioning System similar to what you would use in your boat or your car, but to track people. And like the VeriChip, it would be small enough to implant in someone."

Nathan Issacson is in the early stages of Alzheimer's Disease

Nathan: "I couldn't find my way home, kinda embarrassing moment."

Bobbie Harley: "He already wears a beeper-like GPS gadget and was also injected with a VeriChip. Implanting both devices would give him and his family more peace of mind. Nate can't wait to be chipped."

Nathan: "I'm ready."

Harley: "Are you ready?"

Nathan's wife: "I'm ready. I'm looking for the peace of mind."

Peace of mind, if you'll just receive this implant. Wow! Looks to me like those commercials are working! And correct me if I'm wrong, but it would appear to me that for the first time in mankind's history, that people are not only ready to receive some sort of a Mark into their bodies, but what? *They're totally excited about it*! Can you believe that? And you might be thinking, "Well hey, that's for those crazy people out there. But not me, man! No way! There's no stinking way I'm ever going to go along with this. I'll never take that thing into my body!" Really? Well again, I'll say it again, aren't you glad they took over the health care system? And if you don't think that day will ever come, where our own government will *force us* into taking some sort of a Mark into our bodies, you're wrong. Number one, they forced us into taking Health Care, right? Number two, you better listen to this from congress, where Senator Joseph Biden (who's was Vice President) was grilling then candidate John Roberts for Chief Justice of the Supreme Court (who is now the Chief Justice) and you tell me if there's not plans of being forced, by our own government into receiving some sort of a Mark and implant, into our bodies. Check this out.

John Roberts confirmation:

Joe Biden to then appointee John Roberts: And we'll be faced with equally consequential decisions in the 21st century. Can a microscopic tag be implanted in a person's body to track his every movement? There's actual discussion about that. You will rule on that, mark my words, before your tenor is over. Can brain scans be used to determine whether a person is inclined toward criminality or violent behavior? You will rule on that.[5]

Dr. Katherine Albrecht: I think the real concern that most people have, is that at some point, the government would say, "Line up and get your chip."

But hey, that'll never happen…"You will rule on that mark my words." I don't know about you, but if Congress is talking about implanting microscopic tags into people to track their every move, then my guess is they're probably going to implant microscopic tags into people to track their every move, how about you? And Biden was the Vice President and Roberts has been the Chief Justice for a while now. I wonder when he's going to rule on it…just like he did with the Health Care. I don't know about you, but I'd say it's time we better wake up! Jesus Christ is coming back, and it might be a whole lot sooner than you think. You better make sure you're ready. But here's the point, predictive prophecy, as you can see, is a powerful way to show us that the Bible really came from God. He gets it right 100% of the time and it's happening before our very eyes! And that's why one researcher had this to say.

"Unlike any other book, the Bible alone offers a multitude of specific predictions, some hundreds of years in advance that have been literally fulfilled. This shows us that the Bible alone contains things that only God can know and thus reveals its divine inspiration. Limited beings know the future only if it is told to them by an omniscient Being.

If an omniscient Being is known to exist and highly improbable predictions are made in His name, which come to pass without fail, then it is reasonable to assume that they were divinely inspired. And if the Bible contains such predictions, then they are a sign of the Bible's divine origin."

In other words, you can't have it both ways. You can't agree with some of the Bible's teaching and then turn around and deny its authenticity. Why? Because Bible prophecy clearly presents the Bible as *the genuine Word of God.* And anything short of this is called hypocrisy. And so, it is with the skeptics of the Bible! They spout off bold claims that the Bible cannot be trusted, it's a book full of errors, it's whooped up by man, yet *it is they* who refuse to look at the evidence. But people be encouraged today! You don't have to give into the attacks of the skeptic. You don't have to give into doubt. You don't have to give into one iota of criticism. What we hold in our hands is the genuine Word of God. And that's why, more than ever, we've got to wake up and realize the golden opportunity that God is giving to us. Our world is in a frantic search for purpose and direction and meaning to life. They realize the world is messed up and it's getting worse! And so, they're full of questions like, "Why do I exist? Where did I come from? Where is all this evil coming from? Is there life after death? And is there any hope?" And it's high time that we the Church get busy not just *saying* the Bible came from God, but *showing* the world that it came from God by our diligence in studying it. Why? Because not only is the world going to be duped into receiving a Mark of the Beast into their bodies and sealing their own demise, but there's also going to be false prophets out there, that the Bible clearly warns about, but unless you get in there and read it for yourselves, you're going to fall for their lies as well, like these Christians did.

"You know the term cult really came to peoples' attention, for many people the first time they ever heard the term was back in November of 1978. I'll never forget I was leaving Manila that morning and I was flying to Singapore and I got on the airplane and people were reading the newspaper and everybody was saying, "I can't believe it, how could it happen?"

And I opened the newspaper and there on the Manila Times the headlines read "913 Americans from California Commit Mass Suicide In Jonestown, Guyana" If you remember the cover of Times magazine that week- "The Cult of Death". Telling the story of Jim Jones and the People's Temple in San Francisco.

Jim Jones had moved out to California, established what he called The People's Temple in the Bay Area. Gathered a group of followers around him and began to teach that he was the voice of God, that he was the prophet of God on earth and that he alone had the truth. And he so convinced over 1,000 people here in California that he was the voice of God, the prophet of God on earth that when he told them to move down to British Guyana in South America and establish a commune called Jonestown.

Over 1,000 people from the Bay area moved to South America and we hear on the last tapes where he's telling his followers that he is the messiah, that he is Jesus Christ himself. And when he told them to drink poison, 913 people from California took Dixie cups and dipped it in that vat of grape Kool-Aide laced with cyanide poisoning and they gave the poison to their babies and to their children and drank it themselves and Newsweek had it on their cover the picture of 900 Americans, as their bloated bodies lying in the hot tropical jungle having committed mass suicide following a man who they believed was the voice of God, the prophet of God on earth.

And people said, "How could it happen?" I mean how can you have a thousand intelligent Americans from California follow a man and be told to drink poison and they commit mass suicide. It is interesting to me that the Commander of U.S

Forces who is responsible for going down to Jonestown and cleaning the camp out and bring the bodies back for burial.

When he returned to Dover Air Force Base he held a press conference-he was a Christian-and I'll never forget one of the things the commander stated. He said, "You know the thing that interested us most about Jonestown", he said, "When we cleaned the camp out, we did not find a single Bible in all of Jonestown." They all died, and they were all duped, and there were no Bibles in their camp.[6]

If we don't want to be duped even today or led astray in the last days as Christians, then we better make sure we not only have Bibles in our camps, in our homes and in our Churches but we better get busy reading them.

Chapter Six

Science & Statistics Say So

One day a guy found himself a little short of cash. He went to the zoo hoping to get a job there to feed the animals, surely, he could do that, right?

So, when he got to the zoo there were no job openings available but the manager, seeing the size and strength of the man got an idea. He said, "There are few creatures that are built like you. Unfortunately, our gorilla died yesterday. If we got you a special fur suit, would you be interested in imitating him for a few days?"

So, the guy, needing cash, decided to give it a try. In no time he was quite successful. He was a hit with all the visitors. He was hitting his chest, he was bellowing, he was shaking the bars of the cage. The visitors started saying that they had never seen a gorilla with such intelligence.

One day while he was swinging on the trapeze and feeling a little arrogant; he accidently lost his grip and landed in the lions' den. So, this huge lion comes up to him and gives out this loud roar. The guy starts to back away from the lion, but he couldn't cry out for help because everybody would think he was afraid. He keeps backing up towards the fence hoping to get back into his own cage, but the lion keeps coming at him. Finally, he couldn't help it, he starts yelling, "Help, Help, Help."

To that the lion replied, "Shut up stupid, you're going to get us both fired!"

Now how many would say those two guys should have got normal jobs. Maybe they could have avoided some serious trouble. But that's right, I hope that there is one embarrassing problem that you can avoid as a Christian and that is never ever doubt that the Bible really did come from God. I've been saying that because whether Christian or non-Christian, it doesn't matter, the skepticism and false criticism towards the Bible, and unfortunately, the hypocritical behavior from us, the Christians that never pick up the Bible, is that people are really beginning to doubt that the Bible really did come from God. So, we are going to conclude our study, *Did the Bible really come from God*? We have been taking the 10 lines of solid logical evidence showing us that the Bible really did come from God. So far, we have learned that this is true because:

The Bible says so
Jesus says so
Apostles say so
History says so
Transmission Standards say so
Manuscript says so
Archaeology says so
Prophecy says so

And the last time we found that not only is the Bible full of Prophecy about the future that God gets right every single time, 100% of the time, He doesn't lie, but that is just exactly what you would expect to find if this book did indeed come from God. It contains only the things that God would know.

The **9th line of logical evidence** showing us that the Bible really did come from God is that **Science Says So.** But don't take my word for it. Let's listen to God's.

Isaiah 40:12-22 "Who has measured the waters in the hollow of his hand, or with the breadth of his hand marked off the heavens? Who has held the dust of the earth in a basket, or weighed the mountains on the scales and the hills in a balance? Who has understood the mind of the LORD, or instructed Him as His counselor? Whom did the LORD consult to enlighten Him, and who taught Him the right way? Who was it that taught Him knowledge or showed Him the path of understanding? Surely the nations are like a drop in a bucket; they are regarded as dust on the scales; He weighs the islands as though they were fine dust. Lebanon is not sufficient for altar fires, nor its animals enough for burnt offerings. Before Him all the nations are as nothing; they are regarded by Him as worthless and less than nothing. To whom, then, will you compare God? What image will you compare Him to? As for an idol, a craftsman casts it, and a goldsmith overlays it with gold and fashions silver chains for it. A man too poor to present such an offering selects wood that will not rot. He looks for a skilled craftsman to set up an idol that will not topple. Do you not know? Have you not heard? Has it not been told you from the beginning? Have you not understood since the earth was founded? He sits enthroned above the circle of the earth, and its people are like grasshoppers. He stretches out the heavens like a canopy, and spreads them out like a tent to live in."

So how do we know that the Bible really did come from God? Well, apparently, the 9th line of evidence is that Science says so. What'd we just read? God is not only All-Powerful, and you don't want to mess with Him, but it was He Who created the earth and notice what shape it's in. A circle, right? And this is important to know because the skeptic will usually say something like this when it comes to science and the Bible. They'll say, "Well alright, fine! Maybe the Bible doesn't have historical errors, like we saw with Archaeology, but we know it's got scientific errors, because it contradicts science! Therefore, it couldn't have come from God because God can't lie!" How many of you have heard that before? Uh huh! And then what they'll do is go off and cite as supposed proof of this scientific error in the Bible is that they say that the Bible says that the earth is flat. How many of you have heard that? But what did we just read? No, it doesn't. The Bible says it's *round*. We just read in Isaiah it's a circle! The Roman Catholic Church may have taught that at one time, but the Bible never did! But then they'll go on and say, "Well, the Bible talks about the 4-corners of the earth. Isn't that saying it's flat? Isn't that the same thing?" No. All the "4-corners" of the earth is speaking about is *scope of the earth* not the *shape of the earth.* It just means, "to the ends of the earth." That's all it's saying! In fact, we use this same kind of verbiage today and we don't call people liars for using it. For instance, every single day, I guarantee you, on the news you'll hear the weatherman say something like this, "Sunrise" and "Sunset," right? But wait a second! According to Science, the sun really doesn't rise or set. The earth is actually the one that revolves around the sun! The

weatherman is a big ol' liar! He's full of contradictions! We can't trust him! We don't say that! We know he's just using the same common verbiage to speak about when the sun appears and disappears. That's it! It has nothing to do with lying! Although, it does remind me of the classic saying, "Fool me once, shame on you. Fool me twice, shame on me. Fool me 350,000 times and you're probably a weatherman." But seriously, the Bible may not be a "scientific book" per se, yes, it's not a scientific journal, it wasn't written for that, but it does *not* contradict known science! True science! Why? Because it came from God and He doesn't lie! In fact, you'll be happy to know that not only does the Bible not contradict science but that it's science who is "catching up" to what the Bible has been saying all along! Let me show you what I mean.[1]

• **The Universe had a Beginning**: (Genesis 1:1) Starting with the studies of Albert Einstein in the early 1900's and continuing today, science has confirmed the biblical view that the universe had a beginning. When the Bible was written, most people believed the universe was eternal. Science has proven them wrong, but the Bible correct.

• **The Universe is Composed of Time, Space, Matter, and Energy**: (Genesis 1:1-3) The first three verses of Genesis accurately express all known aspects of the creation. In Genesis chapter one we read: "In the beginning (time) God created the heavens (space) and the earth (matter)…Then God said, "Let there be light (energy)." No other creation account agrees with this scientific observable evidence.

• **No New Matter is Being Created**: (Genesis 2:2) This is called the First Law of Thermodynamics. It states that the total quantity of energy and matter in the universe is a constant. One form of energy or matter may be converted into another, but the total quantity always remains the same. Therefore, the creation is *finished*, exactly as God said it was.[2]

• **The Universe is Running Down**: (Psalm 102:25-27) This is called The Second Law of Thermodynamics or Entropy. This law states that everything in the universe is running down, deteriorating, constantly becoming less and less orderly. Entropy (disorder) entered when mankind rebelled against God – resulting in the curse. Historically most people believed the universe was unchangeable. Yet modern science verifies that the universe is "growing old like a garment" (Hebrews 1:11) Evolution directly contradicts this law.[3]

• **Life only comes from Life**: (Genesis 1) This is called the Law of Biogenesis. Scientists observe that life only comes from existing life. This law has *never* been violated under observation or experimentation (as evolution imagines). Spontaneous generation (the emergence of life from nonliving matter) has never been observed. All observations have shown that life comes only from life. The theory of evolution conflicts with this scientific law.[4]

Vast number of stars: (Jeremiah 33:22) At a time when less than 5,000 stars were visible to the human eye, God stated that the stars of heaven were innumerable. Not until the 17th century did Galileo glimpse the immensity of our universe with his new telescope. Today, astronomers estimate that there are ten thousand billion trillion stars – that's a 1 followed by 25 zeros! Yet, as the Bible states, scientists admit this number may be woefully inadequate.

• **Humans made from earth**: (Genesis 2:7) Scientists have now discovered that the human body is comprised of some 28 base and trace elements – all of which are found in the earth.[5]

• **Hydrologic cycle**: (Ecclesiastes 1:7) Four thousand years ago the Bible declared that God "draws up drops of water, which distill as rain from the mist, which the clouds drop down and pour abundantly on man" (Job 36:27-28) The ancients observed mighty rivers flowing into the ocean, but they could not conceive why the sea level never rose. Though they observed rainfall, they had only quaint theories as to its origin. Meteorologists now understand that the hydrological cycle consists of evaporation, atmospheric transportation, distillation, and precipitation.

• **Jet Stream Circulation**: (Ecclesiastes 1:6) At one time when it was thought that winds blew straight, the Bible declares "The wind goes toward the south and turns around to the north; The wind whirls about continually and comes again on its circuit." King Solomon wrote this 3,000 years ago. Yet it was not until World War II that airmen discovered the jet stream circuit.

• **Air has weight** (Job 28:25) It was once thought that air was weightless. Yet 4,000 years ago Job declared that God established "a weight for the wind." In recent years, meteorologists have calculated that the average thunderstorm holds thousands of tons of rain. To carry this load, air must have mass.

• **The Earth hangs in Space**: (Job 26:7) While other sources declared the earth sat on the back of an elephant or turtle, or was held up by Atlas, the Bible alone states what we now know to be true – "He hangs the earth on nothing."

• **Oceans contain springs**: (Job 38:16) The ocean is very deep and almost all the ocean floor is in total darkness and the pressure there is enormous. It would have been impossible for Job to have explored the "springs of the sea." Until recently, it was thought that oceans were fed only by rivers and rain. Yet in the 1970's, with the help of deep diving research submarines, oceanographers discovered springs on the ocean floors![6]

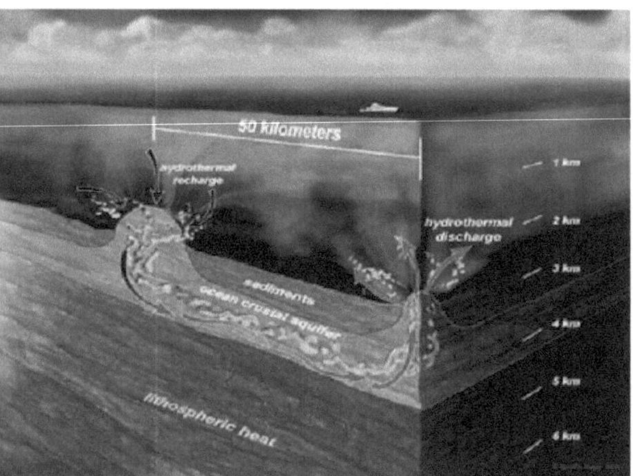

Studies by Andrew Fisher and colleagues have shown that seamounts provide conduits through which enormous quantities of water flow between the ocean and the rocks beneath the seafloor. Image credit: U.C. Santa Cruz. N. Rager. Adapted for use in accordance with federal copyright (fair use doctrine) law. Usage by ICR does not imply endorsement of copyright holders.

• **There are Mountains on the Bottom of the Ocean Floor**: (Jonah 2:5-6) Only in the last century have we discovered that there are towering mountains and deep trenches in the depths of the sea.

• **The sea has paths and channels**: (Psalm 8:8) Three thousand years ago the Bible described the "paths of the seas." In the 19th century Matthew Maury – the father of oceanography – after reading Psalm 8, researched and discovered ocean currents that follow specific paths through the seas! Utilizing Maury's data, marine navigators have since reduced by many days, the time required to traverse the seas.

• **Life is in the Blood**: (Leviticus 17:11) Up until 120 years ago, sick people were "bled" and many died as a result (George Washington). Today we know that healthy blood is necessary to bring life-giving nutrients to every cell in the body. God declared that "the life of the flesh is in the blood" long before science understood its function.[7]

• **Sexual promiscuity is dangerous to your health** (1 Corinthians 6:18) The Bible warns that "he who commits sexual immorality sins against his own body." Much data now confirms that any sexual relationship outside of holy matrimony is unsafe.

• **Disease can be spread by physical contact and the need for Medical Quarantines**. (Leviticus 13) Long before man understood the principles of quarantine, God commanded the Israelites to isolate those with a contagious disease until cured.

• **When dealing with disease, clothes and bodies should be washed under *running water*** (Leviticus 15:13) For centuries people naively washed in standing water. Today we recognize the need to wash away germs with fresh water.

• **Sanitation**: (Deuteronomy 23:12-13) Some 3,500 years ago God commanded His people to have a place outside the camp where they could relieve themselves and bury their waste. Up until World War I, more soldiers died from disease than war because they did not isolate human waste.

• **Atomic Fission** (2 Peter 3:10-12) Scripture states that "the elements will melt with fervent heat" when the earth and the heavens are "dissolved" by fire. Today we understand that if the elements of the atom are loosed, there would be an enormous release of heat and energy (radiation).

• **Light can be divided**: (Job 38:24) Sir Isaac Newton studied light and discovered that white light is made of seven colors, which can be "parted" and then recombined. Science confirmed this four centuries ago, yet God declared this four millennia ago!

• **Light travels in a path** (Job 38:19) Light is said to have a "way" [Hebrew: derek, literally a traveled path or road]. Until the 17th century it was believed that light was transmitted instantaneously. We now know that light is a form of energy that travels at 186,000 miles per second in a straight line. Indeed, there is a "way" of light.

• **Creation is made of Invisible Particles** (Atoms) (Hebrews 11:3) Not until the 19th century was it discovered that all visible matter consists of these invisible elements.

• **Vast Fossil Deposits in the Earth** (Genesis 7) When plants and animals die they decompose rapidly. Yet billions of life forms around the globe have been preserved as fossils. Geologists now know that fossils only form if there is rapid deposition of life buried away from scavengers and bacteria. This agrees exactly with what the Bible says occurred during the global flood.

• **God has Created all Mankind from One Blood** (Acts 17:26) Today researchers have discovered that we have all descended from one gene pool. For example, a 1995 study of a section of Y chromosomes from 38 men from different ethnic groups around the world was consistent with the biblical teaching that we all come from one man. (Adam)

• **Genetic mixing of different seeds forbidden** (Leviticus 19:19) The Bible warns against mixing seeds – as this will result in an inferior or dangerous crop. There is now growing evidence that unnatural, genetically engineered crops may be harmful.

• **Pest control** (Leviticus 25) Farmers are plagued today with insects. Yet God gave a sure-fire remedy to control pests' centuries ago. Moses commanded Israel to set aside one year in seven when no crops were raised. Insects winter in the stalks of last year's harvest, hatch in the spring, and are perpetuated by laying eggs in the new crop. If the crop is denied one year in seven, the pests have nothing to subsist upon, and are thereby controlled.

• **God has given us the Leaves of the Trees as Medicine**: (Ezekiel 47:12) Ancient cultures utilized many herbal remedies. Today, modern medicine has rediscovered what the Bible has said all along – there are healing compounds found in plants.

• **Olive oil and Wine Useful on Wounds** (Luke 10:34) Jesus told of a Samaritan man, who when he came upon a wounded traveler, he bandaged him – pouring upon his wounds olive oil and wine. Today we know that wine contains ethyl alcohol and traces of methyl alcohol. Both are good disinfectants. Olive oil is also a good disinfectant, as well as a skin moisturizer, protector, and soothing lotion. This is common knowledge to us today. However, did you know that during the Middle Ages and right up till the early 20th century, millions died because they did not know to treat and protect open wounds?

• **Laughter promotes physical healing** (Proverbs 17:22) Recent studies confirm what King Solomon was inspired to write 3,000 years ago, "A merry heart does good, like medicine." It is now known that laughter reduces levels of certain stress hormones, which helps bring balance to our immune system, and this helps our body fight off disease.[8]

How many of you would say the Bible not only does not contradict science, but it's science that's been catching up to what the Bible has been saying all along? And yet, this is another thing the skeptics do. They not only *ignore* the evidence, but they act like being a Christian and a scientist doesn't mix! They act like only intellectually inept people become Christians! You could never understand "true" science like us! Really? Well what they don't tell you is that many of the first and the greatest scientists of all time were Christians! Men such as Johannes Kepler, Blaise Pascal, Isaac Newton, Robert Boyle, Michael Faraday, William Thomson Kelvin, and even Albert Einstein believed in the existence of a God and said:

"I want to know how God created this world, I am not interested in this or that phenomenon, in the spectrum of this or that element. I want to know His thoughts; the rest are details."

And he was fond of two sayings, "God does not play dice," and "Science without religion is lame, religion without science is blind." In other words, they can co-exist. They can work together. Why? Because God doesn't lie and He doesn't contradict accurate true science! In fact, neither do the skeptics tell you what they do to people who disagree with their faulty science. Let's take a look at that.

Christian Scientists who were Fired

Roger Dehart, science teacher at Burlington-Edison high school near Seattle, Washington, was told he could not inform students of errors in the textbooks by passing out articles from current science journals.

Kevin Haley, biology teacher at Oregon Community College lost his job for exposing errors in the textbooks.

William Dembski, was fired by Baylor University because he advocated intelligent design.

Forrest Mims, was a science writer for 20 years. He published in *National Geographic*, *Science Digest*, *The American Journal of Physics*, and 60 magazines and newspapers. He was denied a job as writer for *Scientific American* because he was a creationist.

Rod LaVake, of Faribault, Minnesota, was a biology teacher who was reassigned simply because he doubted Darwin's theory.

Dean Kenyon, was a tenured professor at the San Francisco State University and wrote books for years about how wonderful evolution was. But then one day he got converted and they fired him. But he said you can't fire me I've got 20 years. So they said okay and put him in as a lab assistant washing test tubes. He then had to go through a whole big lawsuit just to get his job back, simply because he doubted Darwin's theory.

I don't know about you but that doesn't sound very scientific to me of those guys, right? I mean, you can't even discuss an alternative without getting fired, even when science is saying you need to? What, are you trying to hide? Who's the one being ignorant and biased and close-minded now? But you might be thinking, 'Well okay, maybe those scientists aren't very open-minded, that's not good science, but I know of something that the Bible gets wrong concerning science! Earlier you talked about the how the people in the Bible lived about 900 years old! That's ridiculous! How can you call that scientific?" Well maybe you just need to keep reading your Bible and trust God. Because we know even today that, yes, it's scientifically possible for people to live that long. Let me show you what I mean.

Genesis 1:6-8 "And God said, let there be an expanse between the waters to separate water from water. So, God made the expanse and separated the water under the expanse from the water above it. And it was so. God called the expanse sky. And there was evening, and there was morning – the second day."

According to the Bible, when God created the sky (or the Atmosphere), He did so by placing an "expanse between the waters that were *on the earth* from the waters that were in the *upper atmosphere*." And it's in this text that gives us a clue about pre-flood conditions of the world, and how there was a canopy of water that surrounded the earth's upper atmosphere. Now here's the point. This would not only explain why there was so much water from above when it rained, and why animals and all of life got large, but it also explains why and how people could live for, yes, even for 1,000 years.

"What most people don't realize is that a water canopy surrounding the earth's upper atmosphere would have provided the perfect conditions for people to live such long-life spans, and this is because they would have been protected from the harmful radiation that beats down upon us from the sun and shortens our life spans.

You see, the sun not only emits light, but it also emits harmful radiation in the form of X-rays, ultraviolet rays, gamma rays, etc., just like you get in a doctor's office. And lest you think this isn't harmful, this is why they proceed to give you a lead-lined vest and then the doctors proceed to run out of the room. X-rays might work great to see the inside of you, but prolonged exposure could mean the death of you!

And this is what's going on every single day with the sun. Even though we may not see it, we're literally being "rayed" to death. Our bodies put up a good fight and daily makes repairs, but pretty soon our bodies and our skin can't hold up and so we wrinkle up, shrivel up, break down and die! But here's the point. A water canopy in the pre-flood atmosphere would have prevented this. And this is because lead and concrete are not the only things that shield us from radiation, so does water.

Therefore, prior to the flood, the harmful effects caused by the sun's radiation would have been shielded out and the health and life expectancy of people would've gone way up. And this also explains why when the water canopy did come down at the time of the flood, that the life spans of people also came down with it.[9]

If you look at the ages of people right after the flood, you'll notice that the life spans immediately dropped from around 900 to 400, and then down to 200, and then finally to about 100 which is what we have today. But before the flood, you were just a kid at 100 years old, and we not only see evidence of long life spans in the protection provided by the pre-flood atmosphere, but we also see modern examples of people being protected from the sun and thus living longer life spans.

For instance, studies have shown that there is a noticeable longevity of people who live in steep canyons and valleys that provide a natural shield from the harmful effects of the sun, and then there's the considerable jump in longevity from 1911-1951 when automation in transportation and production moved people indoors away from the sun.

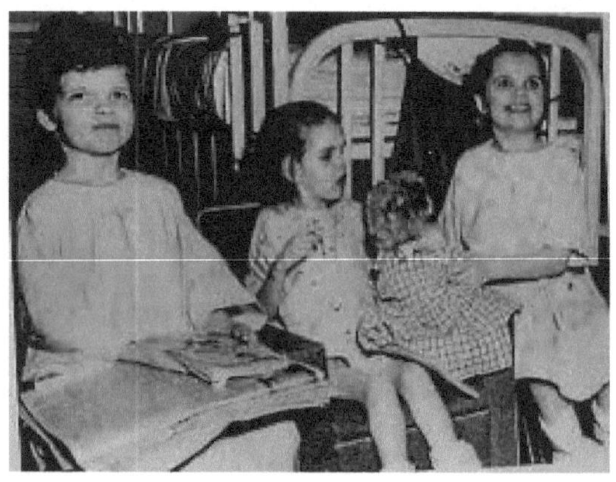

And finally, there's the example of longevity of what happened to the Dickerson children. These children were actually secreted away in an attic until they were teenagers. Pictures of Connie, Gordon and Glenda Dickerson at age 18, 15, and 13 looks like they had literally stopped aging! All the children were still quite healthy and intelligent, but it's obvious that the time they spent shielded away from the sun had an amazing anti-aging effect upon them![10]

In fact, one man, Dr. Carl Baugh decided to take it a step further and duplicate the pre-flood atmosphere and subjected various animals to it, which of course produced some amazing results.

And so promising were his results that even NASA requested Dr. Baugh's research to see if they can utilize it for the space program. And in one of their experiments they did involving three scientists living on the ocean floor in a biosphere.[11]

They stayed in there for about 1-3 months and 'When they left they were all middle aged with graying hair and low libidos. When they returned their hair was clear of gray, their wrinkles had started to disappear, and their sex drive was so increased that their wives complained about it to NASA.'

It turns out that certain glands and organs were 'reactivated' and blood tests showed an unusual level of hormones that are normally associated with the growth in young children.

It was further speculated what would happen if they took this knowledge and built a 'room' with this kind of atmosphere and slept in it for 8 hours a day? The man from the NASA said, 'For every day spent in there, one year would be added on to your life, until you maxed out at 1,000.'"

Those scientific facts about the longevity of life that the Bible talks about are not only cool to know as a Christian, but it sure comes in handy when you run across those people who will only give credence to what they can see or explain "scientifically" like this guy.

"An atheist came to a preacher one time and stated, 'I don't believe anything in the Bible.'

The preacher said, 'You don't believe anything?'

And the atheist said, 'Nothing. I only believe what you can prove scientifically.' Then the atheist continued, 'If you can prove one verse out of the Bible, scientifically, I'll believe it.'

So, the preacher said, 'Okay.' So, he grabbed the atheist around the neck, grabbed his nose, and began twisting it back and forth, back and forth. And pretty soon, blood was pouring down the atheist's face.

So, the atheist exclaimed, 'Man, what are you doing?'

And the preacher replied, 'I was proving the Bible to you. It says in Proverbs 30:33, 'Surely the wringing of the nose bringeth forth blood.'"

Now I don't recommend you give a skeptic of the Bible a bloody nose just to prove its scientific accuracy. But what you can do is point out the fact that it's actually science who's catching up to what the Bible's been saying all along! And this is why you can't have it both ways. You can't agree with some of the Bible's teaching and then turn around and deny its authenticity. Why? Because the Bible not only *does not contradict science,* but it even shares scientific data *long before modern science has even figured it out* and that proves that it's *the genuine Word of God*! And anything short of this is called hypocrisy!

The **10th line of logical evidence** showing us that the Bible really did come from God is that **Statistics Says So**.

1 Peter 1:23-25 "For you have been born again, not of perishable seed, but of imperishable, through the living and enduring word of God. For, "All men are like grass, and all their glory is like the flowers of the field; the grass withers and the flowers fall, but the Word of the Lord stands forever." And this is the word that was preached to you."

So how do we know that the Bible really did come from God? Well, apparently, the 10th line of evidence is that Statistics say so. What'd we just read? God's Word, the Bible is going to stand forever! Why? Because statistically, even though one for one, men will come, and men will go, just like the flowers of the field, God's Word is never going to pass away! Why? Because it came from God and no power on hell or earth can ever take it away! It ain't going no where! It's going to stand forever! And this point is really driven home when you take a look at the amazing statistics concerning the Bible. It proves again that it came from God and there's no way man could ever whoop it up, let alone try to destroy it. Let's take a look at the amazing characteristics of the Bible again.

1. Written over a 1,500-year span.
2. Written over 40 generations.
3. Written by more than 40 authors, from every walk of life-including kings, peasants, philosophers, fishermen, poets, statesmen, scholars, etc.
    a) Moses, a political leader, trained in the universities of Egypt
    b) Peter, a fisherman
    c) Amos, a herdsman
    d) Joshua, a military general
    e) Nehemiah, a cupbearer
    f) Daniel, a prime minister
    g) Luke, a doctor
    h) Solomon, a king
    i) Matthew, a tax collector
    j) Paul, a rabbi
4. Written in different places.

a) Moses in the wilderness
b) Jeremiah in a dungeon
c) Daniel on a hillside and in a palace
d) Paul inside prison walls
e) Luke while traveling
f) John on the isle of Patmos
g) Others in the rigors of a military campaign

5. Written at different times.
   a) David in times of war
   b) Solomon in times of peace
6. Written during different moods. Some writing from the heights of joy and others from the depths of sorrow and despair
7. Written on three continents. Asia, Africa, Europe
8. Written in three languages. Hebrew, Aramaic, Greek
9. And it never once contradicts itself and it has the same message through and through!

And as we saw before, this proves man could never whoop this up! But that's still just the tip of the iceberg. Now add to this fact the incredible scope of the various topics that the Bible covers from law, marriage, government, life, death, heaven, hell, etc. It's not just a one-track story! It deals with all kinds of things! It even utilizes various literary types such as poetry, history, biography, diaries, parables, allegories, etc., and even with all this it still holds on to its unity and it never contradicts itself! In fact, from beginning to end it has the exact same message! Man could never do this! Let's take a look. What are the odds of this?

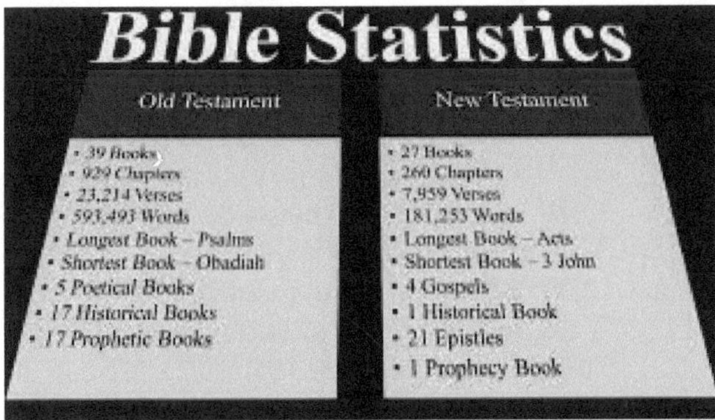

GENESIS	**REVELATION**
1. The Book of Beginnings	1. The Book of the End
2. The earth created (1:1)	2. The earth passed away (21:1)
3. Satan's first rebellion	3. Satan's final rebellion (20:3, 7-10)

4. Sun, moon, stars for earth's	4. Sun, moon, stars connected with government (1:14-16) earth's judgment (6:3, 8:12, 16:8)
5. Sun to govern the day (1:16)	5. No need of Sun (21:23)
6. Darkness called night (1:5)	6. "No night there" (22:5)
7. Waters called seas (1:10)	7. "No more sea" (21:1)
8. A river for earth's blessing (2:10-14)	8. River for new earth (22:1,2)
9. Man in God's image (1:26)	9. Man headed by one in Satan's image (13)
10.Entrance of sin (3)	10. Development & end of sin (21:22)
11.Curse pronounced (3:14, 17)	11. "No more curse" (22:3)
12.Death entered (3:19)	12. "No more death" (21:4)
13.Cherubim first mentioned in connection with man (3:24)	13. Cherubim finally mentioned in connection with man (4:6)
14. Man driven out of Eden (3:24)	14. Man restored (22)
15. Tree of Life guarded (3:24)	15. Right to Tree of Life (22:14)
16. Sorrow & suffering enter (3:17)	16. No more sorrow (21:4)
17. Man's religion, art & science resorted to for enjoyment apart from God (4)	17. Man's religion, art & science in their full glory, judged & from destroyed by God (18)
18. Nimrod (great rebel, king & hidden anti-god) founder of Babylon (10:8-9)	18. Beast (great rebel, king & manifested anti-god) reviver of Babylon (13-18)
19. Flood from God to destroy an Evil generation (6:9)	19. Flood from satan to destroy an elect generation (12)
20. Bow (token of God's covenant with earth) (9-13)	20. Bow (betokening God's remembrance of His covenant with earth (4:3, 10:1)
21. Sodom & Egypt, the places of corruption & temptation (13:19)	21. Sodom & Egypt again (11:8)
22. A confederacy against Abraham's Abraham's people overthrown (14)	22.A confederacy against seed overthrown (12)
23. Marriage of First Adam (2:18-23)	23. Marriage of Last Adam (19)
24. Bride sought for Abraham's son and found (24)	24. Bride made ready & brought to Abraham's Son (19:9 & Matt.1:1)
25.Two angels acting for God on behalf of His people (19)	25. Two witnesses acting for God on behalf of His people (11)

26.Promised Seed to possess the gates of His enemies (22:17)	26. Promised Seed coming into possession (11:18)
27.Man's dominion ceased & satan's	27. satan's dominion ended & Man's restored
28.Old serpent causing sin, suffering, death	28. serpent bound for 1000 years (20:1-3)
29.Doom of serpent pronounced (3:15)	29. Doom of serpent executed (20:10)
30.Sun,moon,stars associated with Israel	30. Sun, moon, stars associated with Israel

And that's just the tip of the iceberg of what's going on with the parallels of Genesis and Revelation. And here's the point. There's about a 1500-year time span between the writing of Genesis by Moses, and the writing of Revelation by John, which means they obviously didn't know each other so they couldn't collaborate. AND YET, they both blend perfectly together, in unity and harmony, telling the same story, 1500 years later? That can't happen by chance! Only God could do something like that![12]

But that's still not all! The Bible alone is unique in its *circulation*. No other book in history has had such a circulation as the Bible. In fact, each year there are so many Bibles sold that it consistently tops the New York Times bestseller list but its left off due to the fact that it would always be listed as the number one best seller. The Bible has been read by more people and published in more languages than any other book in history. Absolutely no other book even begins to compare to that of the Bible. AND yet, the Bible has also survived attack after attack, by people seeking its destruction, like these guys say.[12]

"No other book has been so chopped, knifed, sifted, scrutinized and vilified. What book on philosophy or religion or psychology has been subject to such mass attack as the Bible with such venom and skepticism upon every chapter, every line, and every tenant?

Yet the Bible, is still loved by millions, read by millions, and studied by millions. Infidels for 1,800 years have been refuting and overthrowing this book and yet it still stands today solid as a rock. Its circulation increases more and more and it's even more loved and cherished and read than ever before. If the book had not been the book of God, men would have destroyed it long ago. Emperors and popes, kings and priests, princes and rulers, have all tried their hand at it. They all die, and yet, the Bible still lives."

In other words, it's going to stand forever, just like God said it would! In fact, the big skeptic Voltaire learned this the hard way.

"Voltaire the French infidel who died in 1778, said that in 100 years from his time, Christianity would be swept from existence and passed into history.

But what happened? Voltaire has passed into history while the circulation of the Bible continues to increase in almost all parts of the world. And concerning the boast of Voltaire on the extinction of Christianity and the Bible in 100 years, only 50 years after Voltaire's death, the Geneva Bible Society used his press and his house to produce many Bibles."[13]

But that's still not all. The Bible alone has the ability to transform a life, no matter what somebody's done, no matter how far they've gone off the deep end, the Bible alone can transform a life! You don't get these effects with Secular Psychology, self-help seminars, man's wisdom, religion, or even your own ingenuity.[14] The Bible alone can set you free, like it did for this guy. Check this out.[14]

"1968,69,70,71. Those were years I was in the military. I was in Northern Thailand up close at the border of Laos and Cambodia-kinda in the boonies in a listening station there and had gone through some real traumatic changes. There was also this breaking inside. I just checked out. There really was no redeeming piece of evidence.

There was no way that human existence could be justified. I made the conclusion, stepped over the little picket fence in the na na land that night. Embarrassed. Totally humiliated that I was a human being because of all I've been, all I've seen human beings do. All I've been a participator in. Of course, when you throw off any kind of responsibility of being a human being then you have no restraint and so when you do that, that pretty soon they come in the white jackets and take you away, you know, so they came in the white jackets and of course they had to put clothes on me and everything.

There was no restraint there. No reason to wear clothes if you're not a human being. Umm, but they took me to the hospital in Munich-to the mental ward and did all of their tests and their diagnosis was actually no hope. They decided the psychosis was too deep because I'd seen death close too me. People I loved. People I cared for, in fact I had to care for their bodies-things like that in Northern Thailand and they found that it was really based in this traumatic turn that it made in my thinking and that I would never recover.

Jesus said-Terry I know how you feel. I've seen everything human beings have ever done, but I want you to see the difference in our response to that. You've decided not to be a human being and I decided to become one. And then He took my emptied-out shell and flooded me, drowned me in how He feels toward human beings. It crushed me. It drowned me, and I figured it was just a glimpse of how He feels towards human beings, but it was enough to almost kill me just from His passion toward us as His prized creation, His family. His children. But needless to say, that day they issued a new diagnosis. And where it said no hope before- it said recovering satisfactory."

Only God can do something like that. Why? Because the Bible really did come from Him and it has the power to transform anyone no matter what they've done! Freud can't to that! Hemingway can't do that! Nothing on earth can do that! Man can't do that! But *God can* and it's in the Bible! And this is why you can't have it both ways. You can't agree with some of the Bible teaching and then turn around and deny its authenticity. Why? Because the incredible nature and scope and statistics and power of the Bible clearly presents it as the genuine Word of God. And anything short of this is called hypocrisy. And so, it is with the skeptics of the Bible! They spout off bold claims that the Bible cannot be trusted, it's a book full of errors, it's whooped up by man, yet *it is they* who refuse to look at the evidence. But be encouraged today! You don't have to give into the attacks of the skeptic. You don't have to give into doubt. You don't have to give into one iota of criticism. What we hold in our hands is the genuine Word of God. And that's why, more than ever, *one last time*, we've got to wake up and realize the golden opportunity that God is giving to us. Our world is in a frantic search for purpose and direction and meaning to life. They realize the world is messed up and it's getting worse! And so, they're full of questions like, "Why do I exist? Where did I come from? Is there life after death? And is there any hope?" And its high time that we the Church get busy not just *saying* the Bible came from God but *showing* the world that it came from God. How? By showing them what we've just learned. That the Bible really has the life changing power necessary to not only answer their questions, but to give them hope, and transforms their lives, just like He has done with us. They need to see in us God's Amazing Grace in action! They need to see our lives transformed! We're the only Bible some people may ever see. And what do they see? Hypocrisy? Or the Good News that no matter what you've done, whether you were an occultist like me, or a slave trader like John Newton, God's Amazing Grace is real, and He really can put a new song in your heart, like He did for this man.

"How many of you like Negro spirituals? An old black lady down south showed me something about the negro spiritual and I want to share it with you. You know the black folk down south have more sense by accident than some of us have on purpose you know what I mean?

You didn't hear what I said. Heard an old black lady say, "Son, if the mountain was smooth, you couldn't climb it." Uh huh, think about that for a minute. But then she said to me, "Did you know just about all negro spirituals are written on a black note of the piano?" This is absolutely true.

You can go home tonight and play almost any negro spiritual-just play the black notes on the piano. You look skeptical. Now you can't see it out there, but I want you to watch. We have 5 black notes on the piano. And those same 5 black notes keep reoccurring. You can go home tonite and play almost any negro spiritual. Just play the black notes.... Watch. (Plays. sings) "Every time I feel the Spirit" Just black notes! Watch this. (Plays notes) That's cuz the slaves didn't come to America with doh, ray, me, fa, so la, ti, do-that's somebody else's skit okay. All they had in their musical scale were those 5 black notes.

We know it in music as the pentatonic scale. And they built the power and pathos of the Negro spiritual on 5 notes. When you study music you also come across what are known as white spirituals. Did you know that? And they're white composers who worked with that scale in early America they use to call that the slave scale. Now I'm gonna play for you what some musicologists think is the most famous white spiritual built on the slave scale on just the black notes. (Plays "Amazing Grace" audience sings)

"Amazing Grace, how sweet the sound,
That saved a wretch like me....
I once was lost but now am found,
Was blind, but now, I see"

Anybody tonight know who wrote that song? I heard it. A man by the name of John Newton. But do you know what John Newton did before he became a

Christian? He was a captain of a slave ship and many believe heard this melody that sounds very much like a West African sorrow chant and wrote the words "Amazing Grace" and set his words to a slave melody.

I looked up that song. I believe God wanted that song written just the way it was written. Just so that we would be reminded that as Christians, whether we are black or white, free or bond. In His eyes we are all connected. We are connected by God's amazing grace. I looked up that song at the Library of Congress. I went to the Library of Congress. I looked up that song and where ever you see it authentically printed, you know what it says?

Words:John Newton
Melody: Unknown

I tell the Lord when I get to heaven, I want to meet Abraham and Isaac and Jacob and boy I want to meet that slave called unknown. I recorded that song the way I hear it and when I sing it, I still hear the sounds of the slave ships in the water. I want to see it to you the way John Newton probably first heard it coming up out of the belly of the ship. (Hums the melody)

Sings:
Amazing Grace, how sweet the sound,
That saved a wretch like me....
I once was lost but now am found,
Was blind, but now, I see.
When we've been here ten thousand years...
bright shining as the sun.
We've no less days to sing God's praise...
then when we've first begun.
Hallelujah. Hallelujah. Amen."[15]

How to Receive Jesus Christ:

1. Admit your need (I am a sinner).

2. Be willing to turn from your sins (repent).

3. Believe that Jesus Christ died for you on the Cross and rose from the grave.

4. Through prayer, invite Jesus Christ to come in and control your life through the Holy Spirit. (Receive Him as Lord and Savior.)

What to pray:

Dear Lord Jesus,

I know that I am a sinner and need Your forgiveness. I believe that You died for my sins. I want to turn from my sins. I now invite You to come into my heart and life. I want to trust and follow You as Lord and Savior.

In Jesus' name. Amen.

Notes

Chapter 1 *The Bible Says So*

1. *Percentage of Homes with Bibles*
   https://www.christianpost.com/news/poll-americans-own-many-bibles-but-rarely-read-them-71823/
2. *Stats on What Christians Believe*
   http://www.slate.com/articles/health_and_science/human_nature/2014/12/creationism_poll_how_many_americans_believe_the_bible_is_literal_inerrant.html
3. *Benny Hinn*
   http://prophecynewsreport.com/end-times/signs-of-the-end/social-depravity/benny-hinn-false-prophecies-homosexuals-castro-appearance-of-jesus/
   http://www.biblelight.net/tbn.htm
4. *Pat Robertson*
   https://video.search.yahoo.com/search/video;_ylt=Awr9BNytt8dayTQAzhZXNyoA; _ylu=X3oDMTByNWU4cGh1BGNvbG8DZ3ExBHBvcwMxBHZ0aWQDBHNlYwNzYw--?p=interview+of+benny+hinn+and+pat+robertson&fr=tightropetb#id=6&vid=080f578d7c7cd9a2cf1c663b771f35ab&action=view

Chapter 2 *Jesus & the Apostles Say So*

1. *Who was Jesus*
   https://www.allaboutjesuschrist.org/who-is-jesus-n.htm
2. *Oracle of Delphi*
   https://www.coastal.edu/intranet/ashes2art/delphi2/misc-essays/oracle_of_delphi.html
3. *Bashar*
   https://lazaris01.worldsecuresystems.com/about
4. *Jane Roberts*

https://en.wikipedia.org/wiki/Jane_Roberts
5. *Camora*
http://www.bible.ca/mor-camora.htm
6. *Occult Symbols*
https://www.ranker.com/list/mormon-satanism-similarities/jacob-shelton
7. *Nick Vujicic*
https://www.attitudeisaltitude.com/speaker/nick-vujicic/

Chapter 3 *History and Transmission Say So*

1. *Sir David Dalrymple*
http://www.islamic-awareness.org/Bible/Text/citations.html
2. *Brian Edwards*
Email Story – Source Unknown
3. *Charles Russell*
https://www.britannica.com/biography/Charles-Taze-Russell
4. *Lorri MacGregor*
https://www.youtube.com/watch?v=PM07qLc8p9M
5. *Joan Cetnar*
https://www.youtube.com/watch?v=DiBb1J2vYBw
6. *David Riccaboni*
http://www.blogtalkradio.com/healingxoutreach/2012/04/14/btr-guest-former-jehovahs-witness-overseer-david-riccaboni
7. *Ellen G. White*
https://en.wikipedia.org/wiki/Ellen_G._White

Chapter 4 *Manuscripts and Archeology Say So*

1. *Cave 7*
http://www.british-israel.ca/Mark.htm
2. *Dead Sea Scrolls*
https://www.deadseascrolls.org.il/learn-about-the-scrolls/introduction? locale=en_US
3. *Frederick Kenyon*
https://www.christianity.com/church/church-history/timeline /1901-2000/death-of-bible-backing-archaeologist-kenyon-11630804.html

4. *Flood legends*
https://en.wikipedia.org/wiki/List_of_flood_myths

Chapter 5 *Bible Prophecy Says So*

1. *Daniels prophecy – 4 empires*
https://www.ancient.eu/Nebuchadnezzar_II/
http://www.emmanuelenid.org/images/sermon-archive-pics/Medo-Persian_Empire_Appendix_6_Lesson_5.pdf
https://www.ancient.eu/article/94/the-hellenistic-world-the-world-of-alexander-the-g/
2. *Destruction of Nineveh*
http://en.wikipedia.org/wiki/Battle of Nineveh (612 BC)
3. *Tyre*
https://www.ancient.eu/Tyre/
4. *Healthlink RFID*
https://www.youtube.com/watch?v=W0cqbDC7wa0
5. *Joe Biden talks to John Roberts on RFID chip*
https://askmarion.wordpress.com/2012/07/03/rfid-chip-for-all-americans-in-2013-as-part-of-obamacare-see-biden-telling-fed-judge-he-will-have-to-rule-on-implanted-microchips/
6. *Jim Jones*
https://www.history.com/this-day-in-history/mass-suicide-at-jonestown
https://www.today.com/news/under-spell-jim-jones-inside-tragedy-jonestown-massacre-t109982

Chapter 6 *Science & Statistics Say So*

1. *Round Earth*
https://christiananswers.net/q-eden/edn-c015.html
2. *1st Law of Thermodynamics*
https://en.wikipedia.org/wiki/Laws_of_thermodynamics#First_law
3. *2nd Law*
https://en.wikipedia.org/wiki/Laws_of_thermodynamics#First_law
4. *Biogenics*
https://sciencing.com/theory-biogenesis-5419233.html

5. *Humans from dust*
https://answersingenesis.org/human-body/from-dust-to-dust/
6. *Springs under the Ocean*
http://www.icr.org/article/scientists-describe-jobs-springs-sea/
7. *Blood*
https://creation.com/life-is-in-the-blood
8. *Laughter*
http://www.eternal-productions.org/101science.html
http://www.godandscience.org/apologetics/sciencefaith.html
9. *Canopy*
https://www.gotquestions.org/canopy-theory.html
10. *Dickerson Children*
http://www.genesispark.com/exhibits/early-earth/long-lived-humans/
11 *Dr. Baugh*
http://www.keelynet.com/biology/baugh.htm
12. *Bible Truth*
https://www.compellingtruth.org/Bible-Word-of-God.html
13. *Voltaire*
http://www.god-did-it.com/apologetics-use-of-voltaire-lying-for-jesus/
14. *Truth of Bible*
https://www.compellingtruth.org/why-study-Bible.html
15. *Amazing Grace*
http://www.karmatube.org/videos.php?id=1312

Chapter One
The Bible Says So

Study

1. What percentage of homes in America have at least one Bible?

   92%

2. Give two reasons Pastor Billy believes very few people even read their Bibles.

   a century or more of skepticism &
   false criticism

3. What percentage of Christians say the Bible has errors in it?

4. What do skeptics assume about the Bible?

5. How many times is the phrase “Saith the Lord” found in the Bible?

6. Pastor Billy gives us nine amazing facts about the Bible. List four of them.

7. Who was Michael Nostradamus?

8. What type of entity did Nostradamus admit helped him in his understanding of things?

9. What percentage of Christians said they had consulted a medium or spiritual advisor within the past month?

10. What does Deuteronomy 18 say we should do concerning false prophets?

11. Who was the false prophet who predicted the Rapture would occur on May 21, 2011?

12. What false prophecy did Benny Hinn make during the mid 90's concerning homosexuality?

13. What false prophet claimed God told him Mitt Romney would win the 2012 election?

14. What should the Church do to these false prophets?

Chapter Two

Jesus and The Apostles Say So

Study

1. In Matthew 4:1-11, what did Jesus use against satan?

2. What are the seven things Jesus taught about scripture?

3. To deny that the Bible is the Word of God, one has to reject the ______________________________ of Christ.

4. Name four secular sources (outside the Bible) that verify the existence of Jesus.

5. How many miracles did Mohammed, Confucius and Buddha perform?

6. In John 20:26-28, which Apostle made the claim that Jesus was God?

7. Who does Colossians 1:15-16 tell us is the Creator?

8. What is the interpretation of 2 Peter 1:20-21 for the term “carried along”?

9. What is the occult process by which a writer is taken over by a spirit, who then causes the writer to write down words on a piece of paper, without the use of their will?

10. What techniques did Joseph Smith use to get his "new and improved" supposed revelation of Jesus Christ?

11. What technical term is used for specialized writings that had the authority of God?

12. What did the Apostle Peter call the Apostle Paul's writings?

13. What does Revelation 22:18-19 warn about concerning Scripture?

14. Who was the only Apostle to die from a natural death?

15. Explain the difference between the Apostles and Joseph Smith concerning what they believed.

Chapter Three
History & Transmission Say So

Study

1. How many times did the early Church fathers cite the New Testament in their writings?

2. If every New Testament was destroyed, name a way we could reconstruct it.

3. Name the six filters that were applied when deciding which books to put in the Bible.

4. What fairly recent book stirred up the conspiracies of the "lost books"?

5. What was the source of the "Jesus had a wife" lie?

6. Name the evidences that refute that source.

7. The so-called "lost books" of the Bible were not "lost". They were ____________________.

8. What are the two reasons the Catholic Church put the Apocrypha in their Bible?

9. The Catholic doctrine of purgatory is not only ludicrous, it's _______________________________.

10. Why do the Catholics remove the 2nd Commandment?

11. Most people who doubt the authority of the Bible have never even _______________ it, much less ____________________it.

12. Because of long life spans and genealogy, what three men covered the first 2157 years of history?

13. What happened to a Jewish manuscript that was found to contain even one error?

14. What is the name of the Jehovah's Witness "Bible" and what type of men did the translation?

15. The Seventh Day Adventist "Bible" is based mainly on the teachings of _______________________________.

Chapter Four

Manuscripts & Archeology Say So

Study

1. What were the early Churches encouraged to do when they received the Apostles letters?

2. Concerning Plato's writings, how many years from the original is the earliest copy and how any are there?

3. Concerning the New Testament, how many years from the original are the earliest copies and how many are there?

4. What types of variances were found in the Dead Sea Scrolls from what we have in our Bible today?

5. About how many historical accounts of the flood are found throughout the world?

6. What discovery verified that writing did in fact exist in Moses' time?

7. What discovery in Syria in the 1970's verified the Biblical account of the Patriarchs?

8. Skeptics claim the story of Sodom & Gomorrah is not true. Is there archeological evidence that proves otherwise? What is it?

9. Thanks to the discoveries of archaeologists, we now know that the Hittites were a real people and even now have records of over ____________ years of their civilization, just like the Bible states.

10. Name four Biblical battles that have been verified by various sources.

11. What have archeologists found at the bottom of the Red Sea that verifies the Exodus, just as the Bible stated?

12. Name three things found by archeologist Bob Cornuke that verifies the story of the Exodus.

13. What artifact did Italian archeologists find in 1961 that verified the existence of Pontius Pilate?

14. What archeological evidence has been found to verify The Book of Mormon? (hint: rhymes with zero)

Chapter Five
Bible Prophecy Says So

Study

1. When God makes a prediction in the Bible, what percentage does He get right?

2. The Book of Daniel predicted the rise and fall of four empires. What excuse do the skeptics use to deny that this came from God?

3. Name two nations that the Bible predicted would fall with specific prophecies that happened exactly as the Bible said it would.

4. Pastor Billy lists just 30 of the prophecies fulfilled by Jesus, how many more were there?

5. What is the mathematical probabilities that one person could fulfill just eight prophecies in one lifetime?

6. List five things concerning Israel that have been fulfilled recently that were predicted by the Bible?

7. What percentage of the Bible deals with predictive prophecy?

8. Revelation 13 tells us of some kind of Mark that people would be required to take. Do we see any signs of this coming to pass and what might it be?

9. We can know that the Bible really did come from God because it contains knowledge that only ___________ would know.

10. The skeptics always deny the divinity of the Bible, yet what do they fail to do?

Chapter Six
Science & Statistics Say So

Study

1. The skeptics claim that the Bible says the earth is flat. What scripture tells us that its round?

2. Name four ways science has proven the Bible to be correct.

3. What happens to teachers and professors who point out errors in the textbooks?

4. According to Genesis 1:6-8, what did God do to separate the waters below and the waters above?

5. In what way would the water canopy explain the long life spans found in the Bible?

6. How many years was the span from the writing of Genesis to the writing of Revelation?

7. What best seller is left off the New York Times Best Seller List?

8. What did Voltaire say about the Bible?

9. What book was printed long after Voltaire's death using his own press and home?

10. The incredible nature, scope, statistics and power of the Bible clearly show that what we hold in our hand is the genuine ___________________________.